Move Over Mountain

DATE DUE

Move Over Mountain

*The agonizing confessions of a middle-class housewife
in search of peace of mind.*

Nancy Life

BETHANY FELLOWSHIP, INC.
Minneapolis, Minnesota

Move Over, Mountain
by Nancy Life

Library of Congress Catalog Card Number 74-31682

ISBN 0-87123-375-4

Copyright © 1975
Bethany Fellowship, Inc.
All Rights Reserved

Published by Bethany Fellowship, Inc.
6820 Auto Club Road, Minneapolis, Minnesota 55438

Printed in the United States of America

*This book is dedicated to
my own dear Rich Life, my husband,
who indeed made my life rich
in many blessings and much happiness*

THE LIFE FAMILY

Jim, Rich, Amy, Nancy, Craig

Preface

*"I shall not die, but live, and declare the works of the
Lord."*—Ps. 118:17

I came home from the long trip to Iowa that morning
about two years ago tired enough to barely say hello to my
husband, Rich, before I climbed into bed for some overdue
sleep. Rich stayed home with the children while I went with
the group from church to a Full Gospel Business Men's
Fellowship meeting where our minister had spoken. It was a
wonderful trip full of spiritual food and a lot of fun
fellowship, but I was so tired that all I could think of was
sleep. I'd share everything with Rich later.

I had no sooner laid my head down and begun to relax
when thoughts began to rush through my mind at record
pace. Try as I did, I couldn't relax enough to get to sleep.
The thoughts were forming an outline of the story of my
life, and they were coming so fast that I jumped out of bed
and grabbed a pencil and paper. It wasn't long before I had
it all down, including chapter titles.

I felt newly invigorated, freshly awake as if I had had
several hours of sleep instead of several hours of
sleeplessness. There was also a special closeness to God
that is hard to explain, and I could feel His glow all about
me. Then I saw a vision—it was a book being extended from
one hand to another. That's all I saw, just the two hands and

the book. And then God spoke to my heart about the purpose of this book and how it should glorify Him. My joy soared and I praised the Lord in His goodness to me. That I might in some small way be a part of this vision was too much for me to keep to myself. I bounded out of bed, paper and pencil flying, and ran to tell my husband. He took one look at me and asked what had happened. "You look so different," he said, "All aglow somehow."

God's timing was something I didn't know too much about then in February of 1972, nor did I know much about spiritual warfare. I was to learn a lot about both in the next two years before I actually sat down to begin the writing of this book based on that original outline. In the meantime, there was barely a day that went by when I didn't think about this book and feel a twinge of guilt for not beginning it; but for a number of reasons, the time wasn't right and I wasn't ready— and neither was God. I don't know why God sometimes gives us a vision so far ahead of the goal, but He does, and we dare not proceed out of His schedule.

It hasn't been easy pulling out old memories, old hurts, and old mistakes. There were times when I'd find myself reacting in the present about things that were in the past. Each time either my husband or I would recognize this happening, we would pray together, and the heaviness would lift and the oppression would leave. Each time the battle would be more easily recognized and then more speedily won. When God sets you upon a task, the enemy always attacks to destroy God's purpose. But God gave us power over *all* the power of the enemy, and that is what the story in this book is all about.

This book is also about the kind of faith that moves mountains-- the mountains that confront every one of us in the form of problems, fears, guilt, and burdens.

In a Bible study group several years ago we read Matthew 17:20, "If you have faith as a mustard seed, you shall say to this mountain, 'Move, from here to there,' and it shall move; and nothing shall be impossible to you."

"That's the kind of faith I want—the kind that moves mountains," I said excitedly, discovering it for the first time.

A woman on the other side of the room laughed openly. "You mean you *actually* believe you can move mountains?" she scoffed. "That's ridiculous. No one can *move mountains.*"

"That's what God's Word says, and I believe it. I don't care if it doesn't make any sense." I shot back quickly.

It was a real turning point in my life. God honored my belief in the truth of His Word, and the mountains of problems began to move in miraculous ways as I hungered after this promise of a man called Jesus. There were times when my life was so dark that death seemed the only way out, but then Jesus came and showed me that "nothing is impossible" with Him.

As you read this testimony to His transforming power in my life, I hope you will see that there is no mountain in your life that is too big to be removed with God's help. I pray that your faith in God may be so activated that, through Jesus, you will say to all of your obstacles and burdens, "Move over, Mountain." It is not my word, but His word. My testimony is just a witness to that.

Nancy Life

Table of Contents

CHAPTER 1

Born of the Flesh

"That which is born of the flesh is flesh; and that which is born of the Spirit is spirit."—John 3:6

"I don't care what you say. This time you're not going to stop me. I've had enough and I can't stand it anymore. I can't! I can't!"

Was that my mother's voice screaming from her bedroom? I ran to her door to see what was going on. My mother was standing at the open window of our apartment, one foot on the ledge, and my father had his hands on her arms trying to pull her into the room.

"Now stop it! Nancy will hear you. Come, and let's talk this over."

"Talk, talk. What good will that do? You don't love me—you've never loved me. I can't bear it anymore. I don't want to live. Let me go. Let me jump!" Her screams filled the room. "You can have your women, your liquor—everything! Let me go!"

Horror took hold of my young mind. My mother wanted to leave me because my father was making her unhappy. What did it all mean? Women? Liquor? Tears tumbled down my cheeks. I was frightened—panic-stricken. My whole face grew hot and my body numb. I was six years old and living my first nightmare.

Forcing myself to move—to think—I ran into my bedroom and grabbed some toys, taking them into the bathroom across the hall. I closed and locked the door, clinging to my toys for security. That's all I remember. I don't remember being calmed or comforted. Maybe my parents tried, but how do two unhappy, tortured people comfort their only child when they cannot even comfort each other?

My mother came away from the window eventually, but she never stopped screaming for love, and my father never stopped running . . . and it was many years before I was comforted.

*   *   *

My poor parents. I don't remember them ever being really happy. There was always some kind of turmoil—visible or invisible— but always obvious.

Until I was ten years old my father headed the public relations department at a large eastern university, taking a few months out for government work during the war. He was often away from home and, as the years went on, his absences were more and more frequent. He was an intellectual introvert—hard to communicate with and too deeply involved in a life that didn't belong to us.

My mother was a contrast: Once beautiful, she was soon torn by tensions and frustrations that easily surfaced into scenes of crying and hysteria. Unable to cope with my father's absences and stony silence at home, she was frequently ill. Her unfulfilled need for love and attention often drove her into physical and emotional battles she ultimately fought alone.

Opposites often attract, and as far as my parents were concerned, there couldn't have been two people more unalike. I remember my father as being a proud, distant person—self-contained to the point of selfishness typical of his English heritage, and often true of a person so highly gifted creatively. His professional life ultimately became crippled by his dependence on alcohol, or his obvious writing talent would certainly have earned him prominence in his field. Instead, he moved from job to job, rarely finding complete satisfaction or creative fulfillment. Raised in a middle-class Chicago home with two brothers and a sister, he always felt unloved and rebelled against the unrelenting discipline imposed by a mother who felt that God demanded no less. It was an image that hounded him with bitterness through the years ahead.

My mother was raised by struggling immigrant parents who came from Italy to America where they produced a family of eleven children—ten girls and a boy. It was survival of the fittest for such a large family, especially when there was only one bathroom! My mother remembers those growing years fondly, but she must have forgotten the hardships and unspoken tensions which marked her adult years with such unhappiness.

In the abandoned atmosphere of a Chicago speakeasy, friends introduced my father, a crime reporter for the *Chicago Daily News,* to my mother, a pretty secretary, and an immediate attraction led to marriage some time later. And it wasn't long after that that I was born—the only child they would ever have.

My parents were living in New England then, but my mother had gone home to Chicago where I was born six weeks early. I was tiny and frail, but grew to plump proportions by the time my father first saw me. My parents named me after my mother. All during my growing years it remained a source of confusion, so some of the family began calling me "Junior" or "Little Nancy," much to my distaste. I longed for a name of my own.

I was a shy, frightened child, growing up with almost constant sadness in my heart and a knot of fear gripping my chest and stomach. I always felt small and helpless in a world of people I thought were so much better and happier than I. If I found a rare person here and there who also was defeated and pitiful, I gave of myself compassionately, as best I could, with understanding that comes from a well of similar feelings and experiences.

I cried easily, pitied myself, blamed myself, defended myself, and wept openly, questioning a God who would allow such circumstances—at the same time declaring that things always happened for a reason, for the best. But I wanted to know that "reason" and wanted to have good feelings about the "best" for a change.

Those first years I was often sick—always in and out of doctors' offices and frequently in hospitals, sometimes for long periods of time. I actually learned to love those times because that was when my mother smiled to cheer me, and I so loved to see her smile.

When I was ten we moved to New York City. Much of my childhood was spent visiting museums and historical landmarks and even being a witness to history in the making. Living in such exciting towns (we had lived in Washington, D.C., too) and going to good private schools made it possible for me to meet interesting, and sometimes well-known, people; but I was always lonely, always unsatisfied.

In my teen years my father was away from home more than ever and I began a faithful correspondence. I discussed movies, books, politics, and jobs (mine and his now frequently changing). I sought to console him, cheer him: "I'm glad you feel better now. I hope it keeps up. Even though it's a cloudy day, the sun still shines. Look in the science books and you'll see." But I found it hard to find this same cheer for myself.

> Is it always going to be like this with you in Washington and us here? You can't run away from your fears or from yourself. I do love you, but I can't understand you. I've

never really known you. When you have been here (when you lived here), you were either out all night, behind a paper, or sleeping. You can't give material gifts only and expect that to surpass for anyone . . . Come home soon . . . I need a father. . . . Love, Nan.

My mother and I struggled alone—trying to understand our problems, trying to understand each other, and failing most of the time at both.

I knew God had my answers, but I just couldn't find Him. My parents almost never talked about God, and then only in a purely intellectual framework and never as One who moved in a personal way in anyone's life. It never occurred to me to look in a Bible. I didn't know anyone who read a Bible or considered it the true Word of God. It was a book every intellectual had in his complete library, but it was never picked up and read as a comforting friend or a faithful companion. That daily solace was reserved for the newspaper, magazines, or latest novel.

I talked to God and prayed to Him, but He was so very far away, and I didn't know how to find Him. Sometimes the awful emptiness was too much for me to bear. Three times between the ages of twelve and fifteen I took several pills, thinking the amount sufficient each time to send me into an endless sleep, but it was never enough to do any significant damage. Finally, at sixteen I begged to be sent to a psychiatrist because of the deep depressions over which I had no control. For several months I saw a doctor, but she never saw my parents and never offered any advice. I began to worry about the extra money my parents were spending with no results, and so was allowed to stop my visits.

I was an incurable romantic, and my dreams of the dashing, virile man who would sweep me off my feet and take me "away from it all" never stopped. I maintained that everything was happening for a reason, and yet constantly sought to escape. If something was too difficult to live with, if something took too much effort to change, then escape from it. Escape.

A wind that sweeps away the dawn,
And hums a softer, sweeter tune
Will come.

A sea that moves in tempo, straight,
And carries life to fuller, greener shores
Will come.

A sun that shines through clouds, darkness
And lifts each troubled mind to soaring heights
Will come.

"When?" we ask, "oh, when?";
But that word only echoes in our minds again.

(March 25, 1952, age 16)

CHAPTER 2

Bride, Boys, Breakdowns
and Breakthrough

"Hello, my name is Rich Life. Maybe Spurge already spoke to you about me. I'm his roommate."

"Oh, yes. Now I remember," I said as it came to me. My mother had met Spurge in the apartment laundry a few days before, and he had asked her if he could have his new roommate call me. Rich was a nice young man, Spurge had said enthusiastically, and was lonesome, having moved here from Ohio to go to art school. Couldn't he please introduce Rich to her daughter? My mother liked Spurge and reasoned that anyone he recommended must be all right. She gave her blessings to the introduction and Rich phoned me soon after.

"Is Rich Life really your name?"

"Richard is really my name, but the family calls me Dick. I changed it to Rich when I came here to school because I thought it would be an easier name to remember in business. Don't you think Rich Life sounds famous already?"

I immediately felt comfortable with Rich, even over the phone—so much so that we struck up a lengthy conversation that left the two of us feeling as if we'd always known each other. We hung up with the intention of meeting personally the next evening, and that wasn't too difficult to arrange as Rich lived with Spurge and another roommate just one flight up and one apartment over.

The next night, right on time, our doorbell rang and I rushed to open the door.

"I'll get it, Mom," I called out as I pulled my sweater in place and ran my tongue quickly over my lips. (Somewhere I had heard that one looks more alluring with moist lips.) My heart pounded as I pulled open the door.

What a letdown! I had pictured someone completely different. He was nice looking, all right, but he was so young. How could he possibly be five years older than I? I was frankly disappointed as I had expected a mature, man-of-the-world type. After all, as well as the five-year difference in our ages, he had already served a full term of active duty in Korea and was in his third year in college studying for a career in commercial art. And yet he looked like such a boy! I tried to hide my disappointment, and nervously attempted to carry on a conversation. Pretty soon Rich suggested we take a walk. Good idea.

"Would you like to go to a place with booths?" he asked as we neared Broadway. My heart sank again because I thought he had said "booze," and that kind of talk was a little fast even for me.

"Well, I don't know," I stammered. "I really don't think I'd like a drink. Not now anyway." I was trying too hard to sound casual, and I was awfully nervous for someone who had been frequenting nightclubs for the past three years where I thought nothing of lying about my age in order to order drinks.

"But, I didn't mean that, Nancy. I meant a soda, or sundae or something. Gee, I'm sorry." He could tell I was a bit tense, and his smile, stifling a laugh, saved the evening. Then we both roared with laughter.

This began a series of dates during which we quickly fell in love. Only a month later Rich proposed, and we learned how fast news travelled in our small apartment building.

"Nancy, hello, dear. I hear you're serious with the young art student on the second floor." Mrs. Steinberg was having some trouble balancing her packages when she saw me in the front lobby. She was barely able to put her finger out and ring for the elevator, but she was well able to move her mouth.

"Well, we have been seeing a lot of each other, Mrs. Steinberg. He's very nice."

"Nancy, I must give you some good advice, dear. Artists, art students—they're all alike. Very bad reputation, you know. Terribly fast, morally speaking; awfully loose. Do be cautious. If I were you, I wouldn't see any more of him. I'd hate to see you get hurt. Here's my elevator. Good-bye now."

I was stunned. I didn't see Mrs. Steinberg for weeks at a time. As a matter of fact, we hardly knew her, so I couldn't help but wonder why she cared. Rich and I have often had a good chuckle over that one as he was so different: shy, quiet, gentle—far from the immoral playboy she described, and very much the gentleman.

It wasn't long before we announced our marriage plans to our parents. We had met in October, Rich proposed in November, and we planned to marry in August when I was out of high school. It was all very fast for both our families, but no one voiced real objection to our plans. Rich would be twenty-four and I would be nineteen. What could they say?

Actually, when we made our plans it was obvious that with both of us still in school for another year— Rich still in art school and my going into secretarial school—we couldn't afford an apartment of our own. Rich's folks offered to keep sending him a monthly maintenance check we could both live on during the school year, and my folks offered to look for a bigger apartment that we could all live in together for the time being. It was all very generous and helpful—we couldn't have gotten married at that time without either support—but in the long run it only served to strain the relationship between the two of us and both sets of parents.

It was so difficult for me to grow up suddenly, much less adjust to the give and take of married life. I was playing at marriage like a child playing house. I was selfish and didn't know how to give, and my mother didn't know how to give me up! Living in the same apartment intensified the problem.

Those early months were almost torture as there were many misunderstandings with my mother who felt alone and neglected. I thought marriage would give me security, freedom, independence, but instead I felt even more trapped and frightened. I had pictured my husband as my great defender—my shield. Instead, with each misunderstanding, Rich shrank from the conflict and I took on our defense. My burdens alone were heavy enough, but with the two of us for me to bear, it was too much.

My school demanded four hours of homework a night, and I found it increasingly difficult to balance my time properly or even to clear my mind enough to concentrate. Soon I found that weekend retreats into a wine bottle were more and more appealing. But even this added to the conflicts.

Mom couldn't bear to see the evidences of alcoholism showing itself in yet another loved one. The love she, at best, had trouble conveying became more stifled, and her complex fears and insecurities tore at her heart as she saw me cling more passionately to a husband who couldn't strengthen me and a bottle that couldn't comfort me.

It wasn't long before the tension was so great that I announced I was quitting school and going to work. It seemed worth the scene it created, even though my parents did lose quite a bit of money in paid tuition. I wanted to finish school—for my sake as well as my parents'—but I couldn't keep up with the work. I just kept getting farther and farther behind. Escape seemed the only way out.

Even though we were immature we knew enough to see that our marriage couldn't survive if we didn't leave my parents' home and make a life of our own. My job provided enough money to buy some furniture and we found a nice apartment a few blocks away. My father fully agreed with our decision to move, but then he was gone most of the time anyway. Mother, however, was left more alone than ever. I felt guilty, but I didn't know what else to do. We had to leave some time. Escape again.

*　　*　　*

I worked for several months, taking the subway every day to and from my job, and kept house besides. I no longer had a mother to wait on me or take care of my needs, and I was tired. I knew that we needed the money too much for me to suggest quitting, but I wanted to have a baby and stay home for a change. I somehow talked Rich into the idea.

Everyone seemed happy when I announced my pregnancy, but no one was more thrilled than I when I announced my resignation at work. And what better way to play at house than with a real live doll? I entered my pregnancy with joy and no fear of the birth whatsoever. Not only did this prove in my mind that I was finally grown up, but I was also secretly glad that the birth would take place two years after our marriage and well within the bounds of propriety for all those finger-counting friends and relatives!

I went into labor Monday night after our last Red Cross child-care class. It would have been great timing except for the fact that the baby wasn't due to arrive for six more weeks. Rich and my parents spent a very trying couple of days waiting. To break the tension, my mother told the doctor to be sure not to make it twins.

"You'll be lucky if it's one good one," the doctor replied, and with those words sent a knife right through their hearts. The tension was now greater than ever.

By Wednesday the doctor decided that labor had gone long enough and it was time to take the baby. A beautiful boy was born. Though six weeks before schedule, Jim weighed a hefty 5 lbs. 10 ozs. His biggest problem was that he didn't have the usual sucking instinct and had to be force-fed through tubes extending from his nose into his stomach. His weight dropped rapidly. He presented a pathetic little picture, and Rich and my parents were very worried about his chances of survival. For some reason I didn't seem to think the situation was that serious, and I went home only regretting the fact that Jim had to stay in the hospital and all those darling baby clothes would have to wait to be used.

During the long wait for Jim to come home, I rested and tried to regain some of my strength. I seemed to be weaker than normally expected. One afternoon I got up from the sofa and blood gushed from me like a turned-on faucet. I had never felt such terror as I did in those moments.

The phone rang and I was barely able to get to it. It was my mother calling from work to say hello.

"Mom, I don't know what's happening to me. Oh, God, I think I'm dying! Help me, Mom!"

I don't know how I got to the door when my mother arrived, but I opened it and fainted into her arms. Thus began a living nightmare for me that extended literally for months as I struggled to overcome the shock to my whole system. I was physically and mentally weakened by the experience; consequently it strengthened my dependence on liquor.

My selfishness and immaturity were bad enough, but now my moodiness increased and I was beginning to feel trapped in our small apartment. We looked into the possibility of moving into the suburbs and found a beautiful apartment in Westchester County about twenty miles north of Manhattan. It was a "garden apartment" on the third floor of a three-story building and just perfect for a young family. We had two bedrooms, a large kitchen and a beautiful large living room with a fireplace and built-in bookcases. The grounds were spacious and ideal with playgrounds and picnic areas. There was even a nursery school in the basement of one of the buildings on the grounds where Jim was enrolled as soon as he was of age.

Jim was a darling baby, so good and easy to take care of. He loved the school and he loved playing with his little friends as I sat with the other mothers in the yard each day. I was making friends rapidly and enjoying suburban living as much as I thought I would.

And Rich was happy in his job as art director for a large trade magazine and doing free-lance work for another one to boost our income. He had worked a year as a staff artist for the old *American Weekly Magazine,* the newspaper supplement, and was excited about becoming an art director so soon.

Everything seemed to be so perfect—baby, job, apartment, friends—and yet our lives were slowly falling apart. I was becoming more and more depressed and drinking every day, beginning in the late afternoon. Cocktail hour was an important time for both of us, and we did a lot of weekend entertaining which always included a vast choice of drinks. The party atmosphere temporarily hid the underlying tensions, but the truth always surfaces eventually. I myself was the first to know, and when the truth of what was happening hit me, I reacted with guilt, self-pity, and self-loathing. It was a dangerous combination. Soon I was experiencing the desire to kill myself. I finally became alarmed enough to seek psychiatric help.

Weekly I went into town to a county psychiatrist, and daily I continued drinking. It was the same crash program I was on before, only made harder by the fact that I had to dig up so many buried and painful memories for the doctor.

Occasionally I'd get a call from Rich at work asking me to drive downtown to pick him up. He would go out for an early lunch around 10:30 or 11:00 with his office buddies.

They'd make it strictly a liquid diet so, with the room and his stomach spinning, he needed to get home fast. My mornings always began with a hangover, so I had no desire to begin my drinking until late afternoon and I was always able to pick up Rich if he called.

By this time I had quit going to the psychiatrist in town. He didn't seem to be helping me and certainly couldn't offer any solutions to my problems. He just sat and listened to me! Pretty soon I ran out of words.

My alcoholic intake was increasing rapidly. Now my main purpose was far out of the social realm. I just wanted to get drunk as quickly as possible. The number of martinis Rich and I consumed each night were becoming expensive, so I discovered that drinking beer and martinis in rapid rotation was more economical and got me drunk faster.

I cried easily and often, my depressions becoming more dark and more frequent. I felt guilt constantly, and yet had no control over the very things I did that made me feel guilty. I had everything, and yet my also-constant self-pity reminded me that I had nothing. Such is self-destruction in all its strength and horror.

Rich and I had various scenes over these years with each of our mothers, adding to our agonies and guilt. We wanted so much to love them and to be loved by them, and yet they always made demands on us to which we were unwilling to consent or were too immature to cope with. We hurt them when we wanted to help them and comfort them, and many mistakes were made all around that served to divide our relationships at a time when we really needed to support one another. Our fathers usually stood by as unwitting observers of the mothers' struggles to maintain a remnant of control over their rebelling offsprings.

I sank into a deeper depression, drinking more than I ever had before. Soon I was blacking out each night—not remembering how I got to bed, and sometimes waking up with my clothes on the next morning. It's really frightening to realize that you have done things without remembering them, and learning that you were even coherent and normal to those around you. Also hounding me was the returning desire to kill myself—throw myself out of our window. My mother, realizing that something was terribly wrong, begged me to see my doctor. I quickly agreed, as I was more than ready to seek real help.

"Nancy, I'm going to be honest with you," the doctor began after I told him why I was there—why I needed help.

"You are an alcoholic, and I'm telling you that in case you've been avoiding that word. You have to stop drinking completely if you're going to have any kind of a future. And I mean not another drop of liquor—EVER. You have a husband and a baby to think about as well as yourself. I also want you to begin seeing a doctor I know, a psychiatrist who can help you with your emotional problems. I know you can't stop drinking without help, so I'm sending you to Alcoholics Anonymous—AA. They have a good reputation and a fine program to get you on your feet."

When I agreed to his suggestions, he made my first appointment with his psychiatrist friend, and I left with the promise that I'd call AA when I got home. I went home feeling my first real peace in years, completely wanting to set my life in order and to do the right things to bring this about. I was even bubbling with a new anticipation as I told Rich what I was going to do.

When I called AA and found out the next meeting near us would be held the following night, Rich agreed to go with me even though it was a meeting only for alcoholics. I was too afraid to go alone and thought this was why he agreed to come, not realizing that he might want to come for himself.

I'll never forget walking down the steps and opening the door to go into our first meeting that night. I was happy about the prospect of a new start, but I was also very nervous over the idea of confessing to a bunch of strangers that I was an alcoholic. It did not occur to me that they were all alcoholics too and each had gone through the same anxieties at one time or another. But I have found that it's pride that tells one, "I'm unique, I'm different."

When we opened the door to that meeting, we opened the door to an entirely new life from which we'd never completely return to the old ways. That was the beginning of five years of physical sobriety, a new mental health, a better relationship with our parents, a countless number of new friends, and learning to help others by the sharing of ourselves.

When we entered AA, we met one of the kindest, most loyal groups of people we had ever met. Everyone had been through some kind of personal hell and was there to help himself by helping others. It was a program that succeeded by giving—clearly one got back what one gave out and more. There were always some who were not willing to give of themselves and they were the ones who went back to the bottle. They were the ones who didn't grow and mature in the giving of self, and who broke when life dealt disappointments. They were the ones who were not willing to live in the exacting discipline of AA's twelve steps to sobriety that are as much like Christian living as any program without Christ can be.

We had to admit we were powerless over alcohol and that our lives had become unmanageable because of it. We had to make a commitment to turn our lives over to a "power greater than ourselves—a God as we understood Him." Then we began a moral inventory of ourselves, which involved confessing our wrongs, making them right where possible, and asking God to change our defects (this is a continuing process). Praying and seeking God's will for our lives was encouraged. We were then urged to carry this message to other alcoholics who needed our help. (I still carry the AA card with these "12 Steps" on it as a reminder of the wonderful people who helped change my life.)

Rich and I found ourselves joining AA together that night, and I couldn't have been more thrilled knowing that we were together and that one of us wasn't struggling along alone. After the usual three-month waiting period, we slowly began to go out "speaking"—sharing our stories of alcoholism with others in public "open meetings," at which people who were not alcoholics could come with their friends, relatives or spouses. The "closed meetings" were only for alcoholics. Eventually we began taking calls to visit people who phoned for help from home or institutions; and the stronger and more confident we grew, the more active we became.

It didn't bother us a bit when our drinking friends began finding us dull company because we drank only soft drinks and coffee. We quickly realized that our *real* friends still liked us and didn't care *what* we drank. We were making many new friends in AA and our lives were now so busy that we wouldn't have had time anyway for the ones who dropped us from their social calendars. Besides, the new friends were among the most interesting we had ever met and came from all walks of life: the entertainment world, politics, writing field, and big business, among others.

One night I spoke to a roomful of people that included two figures very well known because they each had their own weekly TV shows. Our good friends included a man who had been a star in radio and early TV, a famous sportscaster, a reporter with the *New York Times,* and the wife of a familiar movie star. Every day there was new fun and excitement; and the gala dinner parties we hosted or attended surpassed any booze brawl for warmth, good companionship, and just plain laughs. Rich and I were living higher than any high we'd had through liquor, and both of us felt ready to think about having another baby.

Jim was almost four and I was completely recovered from the aftermath of his birth—if anything, in much better shape all around than I was before he was born. Just to make sure, I consulted my psychiatrist. I was still going to the one I had started with at the beginning of my AA years. (Psychiatrists are notorious for hardly ever finding a patient well enough to be discharged from their treatment, so I had remained on his weekly calendar even though things seemed so much improved.)

My psychiatrist was a little surprised that I wanted another baby, but he could find no immediate reason why I shouldn't. It was another pregnancy we had planned and were thrilled about, but now Jim could share it with us and add to our enjoyment.

This time when the baby started to come six weeks early, I went to bed and things slowed down. A safe two weeks ahead of the scheduled arrival the doctor put me in the hospital to induce the birth. Also different was the fact that Craig was born only four hours later, a rolly-polly 7½ pounds and very healthy in every respect. All our friends who had offered to drive me the twenty-five miles to the hospital breathed a sigh of relief that they didn't end up delivering Craig in their car. So did I!

I went home hardly able to sit up for the long ride— fighting weakness all the way, but anxious to show Jim his new brother. This time mom had a hired woman to live in for six weeks to help care for the baby so that I could rest and get back on my feet. My mother wasn't able to help since she was still working, so she had hired this practical nurse as a gift for us.

I thanked God that Wilkie was there, because a few days later I began to hemorrhage again. This time Rich was home with me, and I wasn't nearly as frightened. It was nonetheless another terrible shock to my system, both physically and mentally, and, although I still didn't drink during the months ahead, I suffered an emotional breakdown that tragically affected the lives of everyone in the family.

Every demon which had hounded me previously (with the one exception of alcoholism) was unleashed and each haunted me with a fiercer thrust than ever before. Despite my friends, despite my work in AA, despite my dear children and a precious but confused husband, I began to sink deeper and deeper into a hellish unreality. I cried and became angry easily, taking out much of my hostility and fear on Rich and little Jim.

One particular afternoon I was haunted by a sinister, dark depression and driven by an angry, hateful fear much darker and more forceful than ever. I was holding a coffee mug when suddenly I threw it with such force that it went crashing through our sliding glass door. I rushed upstairs and swallowed a handful of sleeping pills, fully intending never to wake up. Instead, I found myself walking downstairs, barely mumbling to Rich what I had done, and then passing out for quite some time. I awakened momentarily when my stomach was being pumped at the local hospital's emergency room and then not again until much later when I was home in bed and people were coming and calling to see what they could do to help.

One of the callers was my psychiatrist who lived in the same town. He wisely suggested that he continue to give me office care rather than confine me to a mental hospital. Another caller was the movie star's wife who unkindly suggested that I had purposely pulled this whole "act" for attention. Every potential suicide wants attention, but this "act" and the events leading up to it were not of my own choosing. I wanted a sane, happy, normal life more than anything else in the world. I couldn't understand, when it was so close, when this dream had seemed a reality, why I had lost such complete control, and the dream had become a living nightmare.

Even my psychiatrist couldn't answer these questions for me, and I began to wonder where I could go to find the answers. I knew that I had to have them or I would meet a final destruction and pull everyone I loved down with me. Over and over I began to call on God for help. I finally knew there wasn't anyone else wise enough to answer my questions or powerful enough to lift the tremendous pressures off my mind.

CHAPTER 3

Church Search

Movies were one of our main forms of entertainment. As a child I grew up loving the glamorous make-believe of theatrical life and always enjoyed losing myself in the excitement of the stories on the silver screens. Live theater was fun, too, but not nearly as economical, and I considered the action often too restricted to be realistic. I usually went to the movies once or twice a week, and Rich and I carried this practice on to mutual enjoyment in our married life.

One night we chose a movie called "The King of Kings." We both liked a good Bible epic and this would be the first New Testament story we had seen. Usually Hollywood told only Old Testament stories.

Up until this time I believed that Jesus was a man who had lived, but no one could convince me that He was God. It just didn't make sense. I had what could be described as a typical Jewish attitude: Jesus had been a good wise teacher, but certainly not God himself.

But as I saw this man Jesus come alive before me in that movie, I felt something I had never felt before, and my heart was quickened to each word He spoke. His kindness, compassion, and love were of a depth that I had never seen before, and I became excited when I saw the healings and miracles. Why, this was the kind of God I had imagined all along, though I had never seen Him in action before! And when He died on that cross with such agony and nature was unleashed with such trembling violence, I knew that something big was happening. I wept because I had denied this Jesus. This was my first real spiritual experience, and I knew that something in me had been stirred that had never been touched before.

But life then continued much as before. One day Rich called me from the office asking me to pick him up. He had been told that he was fired because he no longer seemed interested in his job. It was a terrible shock to both of us. Rich had worked there successfully for six years and had even earned their "Man of the Year" award. He also had one of his covers mentioned in Vance Packard's book *The Waste Makers,* and had had some good publicity in *The New York Daily News* and *Daily Mirror* newspapers. But perhaps he had begun to think of himself as indispensable; perhaps he had spent too much time on free-lance work when he was on the job; or perhaps my breakdown after Craig was born was too consuming. For whatever reason, it was the end of a secure job and the beginning of more rough times.

Our problems previously were emotional and physical; now they were also financial. We had two children to support and our own house to pay off. Rich collected unemployment, which helped for a few weeks, and my mother slipped me money from her paychecks fairly often; but it was humiliating not to be able to stand on our own two feet without outside help, and degrading to admit that we had failed.

"Honey, maybe New York has been too much of a rat-race for you. Maybe you should look for a job out of state somewhere, and we could have a new start." It sounded like a good idea then, but my suggestion proved to be just the beginning of another escape—another running away—and it backfired horribly.

At the offer of a job in Cleveland, we packed up and left our house in the hands of a realtor to sell for us. We made plans with a moving company to come in and carry out everything when we notified them. We said good-bye to our family and friends in New York and left for Cleveland, where we moved in with Rich's folks while we looked for a house of our own.

We tried very hard to begin a new life right away, realizing this would be best for all of us, and started going to local AA meetings. But it wasn't easy for two families to adjust to living in the same house—even temporarily. I felt the pressure immediately, and spent long hours crying alone. The house was old and bore many cracks and wrinkles, and I began to feel that same age overtaking me. Little by little I was dying inside.

When Rich confided that the new job didn't hold the promises he had expected, it was too much for me. All the dark emotions I had felt welling up inside suddenly burst out, and one night I became completely hysterical at the dinner table.

My mother-in-law ran to the phone and called for an ambulance while my husband stood in silent shock on the sidelines with the rest of the family, saying nothing and holding our two children.

By the time the ambulance arrived, I was completely calmed down. The fear that I might be hospitalized had made me strong enough to pull myself together. At the hospital emergency room where I was taken, the doctor agreed that the pressure I was under had been too great for me, and his solution was that we move immediately. My husband and I stayed overnight with a friend in town and went back to the old house just long enough to pack our things and get the boys.

Our house in New York had not been sold, so we decided that the logical decision was to go back to our home in New York and manage the best we could until Rich found work there.

There were various free-lance jobs, but nothing solid to count on. It was then that Rich and a friend decided to start their own advertising agency. Rich managed to get a big account from a local amusement park, so he rented an office nearby and we began the risky life that comes with owning your own business. Fairly soon it was obvious that Rich was doing all the work, so he broke with the partner and struggled alone to maintain every facet of the business himself. And you haven't really lived until you've owned your own advertising agency—and begun it without a penny of capital to boot! The thrills were numerous and our nerves took a severe beating as each day posed a new problem.

We had always felt that going to church was unnecessary, but now Jim was getting old enough to learn about God and we couldn't teach him. We chose a convenient Protestant church and dropped him off every Sunday morning for Sunday school instruction. We never thought to question what he was learning, assuming that all Protestant churches taught basically the same things. After all, we reasoned, it was the same God and the same Bible!

It wasn't too many weeks after Jim started Sunday school that he came home with a very embarrassing question.

"How come when I'm in Sunday school you're not upstairs in church with the other parents?"

Wow! How do you answer something like that without realizing that any answer will be wrong? We had no good excuse. And that's how Rich and I began to go to church!

We chose one near our old apartment because we knew some of the people who went there. We attended regularly and I became active right away in the Women's Circles and the annual church bazaar. We both enjoyed the monthly Couples' Club—the people were a lot of fun to be with and the food was delicious! We found our circle of friends greatly increased and our activities broadening. Rich and I joined their Bible study group too.

I wasn't learning anything about this new Jesus I found at the movies, but we were having our first "religious" exposure, so I thought I'd find Him there eventually. I began to ask a lot of questions.

"I don't understand why we have to baptize our babies? What do you mean when you say it's to remove the original sin?" I asked our pastor.

"When Adam and Eve sinned in the Garden of Eden, they broke the communication between God and man and their sin was passed on to mankind. Baptism covers this sin," he answered.

I still didn't understand what my children or I had to do with something Adam and Eve did. I was so sure we make our own mistakes and pay our own penalties.

"Is the Old Testament really true? Am I to believe all of those incredible stories?"

"No," answered the pastor. "They're just symbolic stories to get a point across—to explain a moral. It's always easier when done graphically. Just like the parables Jesus told."

"I thought so," I replied.

We were still going to AA, but with all our moving and problems and new church activities, we were less and less active. Pretty soon I found myself actually restless there. One day I spoke to Rich about it.

"The more I learn about alcoholism, the less I know about it! Why, even the doctors—the so-called experts—admit they don't know much about it. And I don't enjoy being around 'sick' people all the time. It's so defeating—so negative—because you're always considered an alcoholic. I mean, you're never really well. And so many of those people live in fear—some of them downright panic—that tomorrow they'll take that first drink! Honey, I think it *is* possible to recover and be able to drink again normally—socially."

I convinced him. After five years of sober, active work in AA, we dropped out and began to drink again. And we proved my theory to be true for quite a few years.

We had some drinking friends in our new church and a couple of them drank heavily. I remember one girl in particular who couldn't get over the fact that I used to be an alcoholic but that I wasn't anymore. I longed to be able to tell her how it worked, but I really didn't have the answer then. And she needed an answer badly.

Most of our old AA friends decided that we couldn't have been alcoholics before, and more than a few were glad for us. We knew we had been.

I was much more settled emotionally, but there were still periods of strain and stress that were harder than usual. I was still a nervous person, unsettled and basically unhappy. I was at my best being busy and involved. I knew it helped to keep me out of depression.

I had kept up my visits with my psychiatrist as best I could. Although it was becoming easier for me to think of things to say each time, I can't say there was any real progress because of these visits. His training taught that it was his job just to listen and silently evaluate. To this day I can't see how a sick person could find his own solutions merely by talking out loud to a doctor for $20 per hour and up! I began reading books on psychiatry and autobiographies of others who had gone through therapy to see if I could come up with my own answers. I was quite enthused when my psychiatrist told me he was interested in the furtherance of religion and psychiatry, but God was never mentioned by him in our visits, and my bringing the subject up never got anywhere either.

One day he said to me, "Mrs. Life, why don't you look around you and see that there are others who have gone through so much more suffering, have so much more to worry about, than you do?"

"That's true," I agreed, "but when you're going through it yourself, it's your pain and there's no other pain that hurts as much."

He nodded his head in agreement.

We discovered a strain in the budget and decided to sell our house and go back into an apartment. It was too bad we got the apartment before we sold the house, because for several months we paid for both! What began as a thrifty move turned into a frantic shortcut to debt. So, back to the house we moved, like whipped dogs, having to admit mistake and failure again. It wasn't easy, and I might say that by now it was quite embarrassing. Unfortunately, all these moves of ours involved school changes for Jim, who amazingly was remaining sweet and well-behaved through it all. Craig was still very young, so it was easier on him.

Now the going was really rough, and it was obvious we wouldn't be able to hold onto the advertising agency. One big account was pulling out because Rich wouldn't agree to vote their way politically—it was a matter of principle with us. We were in debt because of the moving expenses and paying both rent and mortgage payments at the same time for several months. We made an appointment to see our pastor. We wanted to do things God's way for a change, and we thought he might know what that was.

He really didn't have any answers, but he did pray before we left and asked God to show us His way for us. I don't think that the pastor ever knew it, but I believe that prayer helped to change our lives.

We went home with our problems and waited for the answers. Rich hunted daily through the *New York Times* want ads again, and even looked into a nightwatchman's job in the cemetery across the street from where we lived. They didn't consider him qualified enough!

We were way past our last dollar, deep in despair and worry when I turned on the TV that night. Rich had gone out, so I was alone. I flipped the channel selector and stopped when I heard a voice singing a song that came alive like no other I had ever heard.

Shackled by a heavy burden,
'Neath a load of guilt and shame.
Then the hand of Jesus touched me,
And now I am no longer the same.

CHAPTER 4

Born Again

I had turned on a telecast of the Billy Graham Crusade and sat watching—suddenly too engrossed to turn it off. I considered religious television shows dull, but this one was different. Everyone seemed so happy and really excited about this man Jesus they talked about as if they really knew Him.

Then Billy Graham himself came forward to give the sermon. His words didn't stop with my mind, but went straight to my heart. He said something about problems being solved, lives being changed, and all because of the turning over of one's life to God—to Jesus. He was talking about me, and I knew it. I had a lot of problems and my life surely needed changing. I did what he said at the end of the program and sent my name to his headquarters in Minneapolis, Minnesota, trusting that God was now going to direct my life as He never had seemed to before.

From that time on I considered myself a real Christian, but there was no doubt that God had a big work yet to do in me. There were an awful lot of unanswered questions, and my real spiritual understanding was cloudy. But God honored my commitment to Him and began to lead me in an obvious way into His truth and a living knowledge of Him. There were many detours in the process, though!

The next day Rich found an interesting ad in the *Times*: Art Director for *The Catholic Digest Magazine* in St. Paul, Minnesota. The salary looked good, and we were so desperate at this point that even the idea of moving appealed to us—especially when we heard that the cost of living was so much cheaper in the Midwest. We hoped this would be the answer to a lot of our problems.

Soon Rich received a request to fly to St. Paul for an interview, and he returned with glowing reports about the job and the area. We talked it over and decided that when he was offered the job, we'd better take it. I didn't like the idea of leaving my parents and friends—all my roots—but I knew we didn't have too much choice at this point. I tried hard to look on the bright side and concentrate on the advantages.

I had never moved anyplace before where we didn't already have friends or relatives, and this new experience was very hard for me. I was lonesome and found the adjustment from activity to inactivity difficult and painful. For the first time in my life I found myself hungry all the time. It was a whole new thing for me as I had never had much of an appetite before, and now I was hungry even after a full meal. I was eating three meals a day and then snacks besides. It wasn't long before I had put on fifty pounds and had to buy a new wardrobe to accommodate my new proportions. For the first time in my life I thought about diets (though I never seemed to be able to stick to them), and I was embarrassed even to walk down the street. Where before I had possessed an eye-catching figure, now I caught eyes for reasons that were no longer complimentary. I discovered that buying clothes—which once had been such fun—now included the painful experience of facing a full-length mirror and realizing that nothing—absolutely nothing—really looked good anymore, no matter how smart or stylish. Guilt completed the torture every time I went near the refrigerator!

I realized that I had to get involved in some kind of life in our new town or I would find myself in a far worse state, so I joined everything I could think of that had a nursery in which to leave Craig. Rich had found a church for us that was very much like the one we had gone to at home, so I joined all their women's activities I could. I also signed up at the YWCA for bridge lessons, and that class of women got along so well together that we formed our own club and played bridge together for the next few years. Another activity I enjoyed was bowling once a week in a neighborhood league. I was finally getting acquainted and learning my way around.

Generally speaking, although they were kind and polite, the people were different from those I had been used to in the East. I found out the hard way that they didn't complain or share their problems and didn't expect me to do so either. They were close-knit family people who stayed among themselves on holidays and weekends. They just didn't consider that we might not have relatives of our own to be with. This never bothered Rich, but I had always been used to large family gatherings and I missed this very much.

There are always exceptions, however, and one of them was a neighbor named Kitty. She had experienced a lot of pain in her life and was keenly aware when others were in need. She tried very hard to cheer me up and to show me around town and make me feel welcome in the neighborhood. One day I complained to her that our church didn't have a Bible study group I could join. I had just started to go to one in our church back east and eagerly wanted to pursue the studies of a book I had barely opened. We talked about the neighborhood group that was successfully in progress, but we couldn't go until our children were in school because they didn't appreciate little ones around breaking the train of study. We could understand that! But I had two years to wait until Craig started school, so Kitty had another suggestion.

"I had a couple of women at my door the other day who offered to come to my house once a week and teach me the Bible. It would be great if you came, too. I'm sure they wouldn't mind, and Craig is welcome, too. He could play with Tommy while we study."

"You mean these women don't charge anything for this, Kitty?"

"No, not a thing. They'd do it for anyone who asked them. Isn't that great?" Kitty seemed just as hungry as I was for more of God.

"Boy, I'll say. Sure, I'll be there. What time did you say?"

The two women turned out to be just as nice as I thought they would be to do this for us for nothing. I found out that they called themselves "Jehovah's Witnesses," but this didn't mean much to me. They had a Bible and were willing to answer my questions and teach me all the things I didn't know and yearned to. I assumed that anyone who taught from the Bible must be all right. My knowledge of Scripture was extremely poor, but I retained a strong stubborness about things that I couldn't understand or agree with. In some areas we agreed nicely because of this. The other areas proved the eventual parting of our ways.

They did not believe in the reality of the Trinity—a Triune God—and we had no problem here between us. It was something I didn't understand so therefore also denied. My theory was: If I didn't understand it, or it couldn't be explained, then it wasn't true! To me that was logical and simple.

They also didn't believe in hell and eternal punishment, or in the reality of Satan. Here also I agreed. I had always thought that one paid for his sins in life and made his own personal hell by his mistakes.

But Kitty kept asking them questions about how they would handle certain aspects of life, problems that might arise because of some of their different beliefs—mostly their stand in being conscientious objectors. She got off into imaginary situations, their solutions for which left a lot of questions in my mind.

"You mean you wouldn't kill anyone in self-defense for *any* reason—any reason at all?"

"That's right."

"Well, what if someone was attacking one of your children?"

"Not even then."

"And you couldn't take part in anything having to do with any war effort—not even in an office?"

"That's right. It would still be helping, even inactively, in the taking of another human life."

"Well, what if we had a war in this country," Kitty went on, "and one of our soldiers was wounded and dying on your front steps—begging for help. What would you do then?"

"Nothing. It would still be helping the war effort in general no matter how I looked at it."

That did it for me. I went home very disturbed for the next week. I could accept the fact that they couldn't salute the flag or exchange birthday or Christmas gifts or take a blood transfusion. That was their business even though I didn't agree, but this was so much more. Not helping a dying man—for any reason—was more than I thought was right. If not helping to kill people was done for humane reasons, then surely helping to save their lives was also necessary in God's eyes.

The more I worried about this aspect of their teaching, the more convinced I was that their religion wasn't for me. This was not the kind of love I thought a Christian should have. I went to Kitty and told her just what I thought and that I couldn't study with these women anymore. When I saw them I told them the same thing and thanked them for their time. They offered no excuses and no challenges. Kitty quit soon after. Now I was on my own again. I still didn't read the Bible on my own but depended on others to teach me. It was only by God's grace and mercy that He protected me from a religion that denies the deity of His son, Jesus, without which there can be no salvation. I didn't realize then that denying God's teaching on the Trinity also meant a denial of Jesus himself, for God cannot lie.[1]

During this time, one of my friends from church told me about a group that seemed like one I'd be interested in with my background in psychiatrists' offices. A friend of hers had started weekly meetings with people she knew who had problems and were seeking answers. They thought their solutions lay in getting it all out in the open, sharing experiences in solutions, and searching the Bible and other books for more answers. Two things appealed to me: that I might be able to help other people from my own experiences, and that I would be in a group that offered me a chance to learn something about the Bible.

The women turned out to be warm and friendly, and I felt comfortable with even the most troubled. I was excited about the chance to share in a discussion group, and it was just the right size for the purpose—ten or twelve women at the most. Some had very serious marital problems and others were already divorced, but I could relate from the viewpoint of similar emotional turmoil in our lives in one way or another. I looked forward to every meeting and felt that, although I wasn't learning much, at least I might be contributing something. And I was making more friends, which I enjoyed doing, my lonely days being long gone now.

I was busy again and Rich was doing well at the office. His job offered him a lot of opportunities for the expression of his creative versatility, as he illustrated many different

---

[1]See 1 John 5:7,8, which the Jehovah's Witnesses have removed from their translation of the Bible.

story subjects. Even though the cost of living was less in the Midwest, there was always more to want, and Rich found free-lance work again. We were able to afford some nice vacations in a northern resort. And that was a real treat for all of us. We made a good buy on a used boat which we used a lot since we lived up the block from a lake with a private beach. We enjoyed swimming and fishing and wished we knew how to ski when the long winter months were on us (but we never did learn). The boys were doing well, too. It all looked good, but underneath it all we still had that restless desire to go back to our friends in New York. In time, we thought, the urge would leave us.

My interest in the weekly "share group" lasted for many months, mainly because I liked most of the girls so much. But I wasn't really learning as much as I thought I would. I was especially disappointed that we weren't getting into the Bible after all, and that the discussions centered more around other books and sometimes other religious beliefs than those based on Christian doctrine. I was very happy when I heard that the young assistant minister at church had agreed to come and head the group for us. Now, I thought, I'd finally get my answers and get on with learning about God.

But he didn't use the Bible in the meetings either, and I disagreed actively when he began to exercise too much of what I labeled "dangerous amateur psychiatry." I felt some kind of harm—real danger—that I had trouble explaining, and eventually I grew so restless that I decided to leave the group. I told the others that they'd better be careful—that this was all wrong—but no one seemed to understand. I couldn't blame them. It was only an impression I had.

But God had stepped in again to protect me, as they had just begun to be interested in "sensitivity training,"[2] and I

---

[2]Sensitivity theories are dangerous because they stress man's dependence on man rather than on man's Creator. They also teach the im-

didn't know anything about it then. God knew I wasn't searching for thrills or for something that would put me on a special plane of knowledge above anyone else, but that I was honestly seeking for more of Him and His truth. He knew this because He knew my heart, and He honored this desire with His protection and guidance.

For a number of reasons Rich and I became very restless in the church we had been attending. Neither we nor the children seemed to be learning anything. God had placed such a hunger in my heart for more of Him, and this hunger wasn't being satisfied. There was no talk there of a real and living God, hardly any mention of Jesus, and the busy social flow and heady organizational functions no longer were enough. Rich agreed that we should try another church. We picked one closer where some friends and neighbors went, a church steeped in ritual and stately pomp. Both of us got a big chuckle out of trying to keep up with the service in their prayer book. We were forever a page or two behind and on our knees when we were supposed to be standing and standing when we were supposed to be sitting! Would we ever learn?

Again we became active in their social calendar. This time the boys seemed to be learning something in Sunday school. We still weren't learning anything ourselves, but we wanted to give this church an honest try and made every effort to adjust, always hoping that this would be the church that would have the answers to our questions about the God I was so desperately seeking.

The people were very nice, but three times on three different occasions, when someone would ask what church we came from and we told them, the reply would be the

---

portance of the group as a whole and negate the worth of the individual. Much of this is taught through verbal interplay as well as physical, and here too "anything goes," as inhibitions are abandoned and old standards taken away. The members of this group that remained began to accept the "new morality" through these techniques and eventually followed a course of study which led deeply into the occult.

same, "Oh, then you can't receive Communion in our church."

It was a big blow to me to find myself in a place that would deny me Communion. Even though I didn't really understand Communion then, I knew that Jesus would never have denied me Communion on the basis of my church affiliation (at least I couldn't find it in the Bible), and I had a strong belief in doing things like Jesus did them. No one would reply to this, and once again a church had disappointed me.

I was still empty and I sorely needed direction! But God knew my heart's cry and, true to His promise to those who seek Him, pointed me in the right direction.

Craig started school, and finally I was able to join the group of neighbors and others who met to study the Bible under the leadership of a minister's wife. He no longer pastored in a church but was a professor at a local Christian college, so they spent their summers traveling worldwide. Mrs. Jones, I'll call her, brought the Bible to life with exciting stories of her experiences in different lands through which she had traveled and had learned much of the history and the people. Mrs. Jones believed the whole Bible was the complete and true word of God, and she was the first person I had ever met like this.

I didn't believe everything she taught, but the more tolerant I was of her beliefs and her right to express them, the more I found myself accepting them. She was a patient, simple woman who loved God with all her heart and wanted to serve Him. She was very typical of my mental picture of a missionary: white hair pulled straight back into an austere bun at the nape of the neck, not one trace of makeup to color the face, a rather bulky frame with little feminine allure, and dresses that were too old to have come back into fashion yet and always more than long enough for modesty's sake. I loved her ready smile and her patience with our questions and conversations, which were often off the subject. Frequently we would launch into discussions of community problems, branching usually into the world at large—and Mrs. Jones would sit by pleasantly nodding agreement and temporarily setting aside the Scripture study of the moment.

I loved the stories of her close family life and how God took care of so many of their needs. I was especially impressed when she told about how her children loved their prayers. One child was just an infant when one night Mrs. Jones forgot to kneel by her crib and recite the prayers it was her custom to say out loud. The baby cried and cried until Mrs. Jones realized what the problem was, and then the baby went peacefully to sleep. What a beautiful way to raise a baby, I thought.

God began to speak to my heart about the importance of prayer. I saw how beautifully Mrs. Jones was able to pray before our studies started, and I marvelled at her easy expressions to a God who was so real to her. I began to kneel by my bed every day after lunch when I was alone and it was quiet, and I talked out loud to God about my requests and needs. My words didn't sound as fancy as Mrs. Jones'—no "thees" and "thous"—but I knew God could hear me.

"Help me, Lord, please not to be so 'poopy,' " I'd say, and He would.

"Help me to understand what you want me to do for you. Help me to learn more about you," I'd ask, and I began to hear His still small voice in my heart.

One day Mrs. Jones was teaching from the book of John, and we began discussing what Jesus meant when He said, "You must be born again in order to see the kingdom of God."

"Well, I was raised in a Christian home and always believed in Jesus. I certainly don't have to commit myself all over again when I've *always* been a Christian," some of them said.

I listened, hoping that this problem would be cleared up

for me, too, but the answer seemed to be that one must be born again just because the Bible said so. My mind was still trusting in logic and reason and I needed to understand why, and couldn't. Pretty soon the subject was dropped.

As I prayed my simple prayers each day, God started to move in surprising ways. Rich had changed jobs a few months before in order to raise his salary and go into the field of audio-visual education with the 3-M Company in St. Paul. He was sitting in his office one day when he received a telephone call from New York. A man with whom he had been in touch a long time before was calling with an offer from a division of Prentice-Hall to become one of their producers—similar to the work he was now doing for 3-M. It was a tremendous chance to go back to New York, the longing for which we'd never really gotten over. While he was on the phone someone came in from the next office telling Rich he had a call on the other line.

"Mr. Life, this is Mrs. Henley. I'm with the —— Realty Company and have driven a couple around your neighborhood. They took a fancy to your house, and I was wondering if by any chance you would let me show it to them for a possible purchase?"

We have long since learned that God often moves just this way, "His wonders to perform." Now we find this kind of situation to be almost common when we let God handle our lives. At that time, however, we couldn't believe it all was really happening, and we were more excited than you can imagine.

That couple bought our house, Rich accepted the new job in New York, and we were finally on our way back home.

Just before we left I got on my knees again. "Dear Lord, please send me a Christian friend in New York. I never met any when I was there—not any who talked about you and seemed to know you in a real and special way. I mean, Lord, a 'born again' type Christian. There might not be any there, but please find me one if there is! Amen."

CHAPTER 5

Born Again, Again

Rich and I were standing in our empty house in Mt. Kisco, New York, waiting for the moving van to arrive with our furniture from St. Paul. The boys were in New York City with my mother until we got settled. It was our first day in this new house and we wondered what was now ahead. We were tired and hungry and quietly contemplating our new future when the doorbell interrupted.

"Hi, my name is Joan. I live about a half a block up the street that way. I thought you might be hungry and brought a few things for you."

A few things? Her arms were loaded with sandwiches for us, and milk, fruit, dessert, and a big pot of coffee. There wasn't anything she had forgotten. She went on to explain that our realtor had spread the word about us buying the house, so Joan knew just how many to prepare for and when we'd be there to need it.

"I'm sure you're going to be busy now, but I want you and your family to come over to our house for dinner tonight."

We protested that she had done more than enough, but she insisted. We picked up the boys at my mother's apartment that night after the movers left and came back for dinner at Joan's.

I took one look at the Bible on her coffee table and knew

she was the Christian friend God sent me. He hadn't wasted one bit of time answering my prayer! When I realized this, I asked Joan where we could go to church and she recommended a place called Hillside. I had been especially concerned about having a church to go to right away.

"We don't go there ourselves, but the people I know who do are the kind of glowing ones who have God really flowing in their lives," Joan said.

It was the church that a friend from St. Paul had already heard about and encouraged us to investigate. Joan's words seemed to be a confirmation for us. She also mentioned that she was going to start a Bible study group in her home and would I be interested. Would I? I couldn't get over how fast God was moving us in His direction.

We renewed old friendships and made a lot of new ones as the people in our neighborhood kept coming over with more food and warm introductions. They couldn't have been more helpful and friendly.

Mt. Kisco was a beautiful New England-type area rich with hills, trees, and quaint architecture. Across the street from our house was a large reservoir surrounded by woods—a perfect place for long walks and fishing, even some hunting in season. It was a lovely setting and only fifty miles from New York City. The children made new friends easily and things seemed to be going well in Rich's job. He was producing educational filmstrips, working on all facets of production, including narration and musical arrangements, and enjoying his work in this new field even more than illustration and art direction. I was happy for him, happy for the boys, and happy in our new neighborhood and in the new church.

Hillside was a charming white colonial church set on a rolling hill, trees making a perfect backdrop—a picture postcard setting. It was the first fundamental, Bible-believing church we had ever attended. The people were more than just nice—they were alive! They loved God, they served Him, and they used expressions I wasn't used to hearing. They talked about Satan as if he were real, they used the word "saved" as if they were actually able to tell when someone was, and they often referred to hearing God speak to them as if they really knew His voice. They even got together once a week just to pray. Something began to stir in my heart—something good—and I felt as though we were in the right place.

We hadn't attended Hillside very long before another local pastor called on us. I was alone that afternoon and asked him in when he said that some neighbors, who had heard we were looking for a church home, had sent him over.

"I'm sorry, Pastor, but I'm pretty sure that we're going to call Hillside our church home."

"Hillside! You don't want your boys to go there, Mrs. Life. That's the kind of church that puts a very strong emphasis on the Bible, and too many young people rebel against that kind of approach. We give the young people what they want—what they enjoy. We have a very active youth program and our new building will have much better facilities than we have now—even a basketball court. And, Mrs. Life, at our church you and your husband would be attending with the best people the community has to offer. Why, we even have the Chairman of the Board of the *Reader's Digest* magazine in our congregation!" The pastor actually glowed with pride.

"I'm sorry, but we want the boys to learn the Bible, and I really think that's far more important in the long run than what you say your church has to offer. We've tried those things and they just don't meet our needs; they don't answer our questions. We can get those things anywhere else, but when we go to church, we want to find God."

He looked uncomfortable, I was uncomfortable with him, and he excused himself politely and left with the reminder that his church was there when we wanted to change. I had met the temptations of the world, so to speak, and chosen instead to follow the simple teaching of God's Word without embellishments. I had waited too long to find out more about God, and I wasn't going to stop now.

I didn't think any Bible study could measure up to Mrs. Jones', but I quickly found that this new approach of learning scriptures without a leader and with only a study guide for direction wasn't as bad as I had thought.[1] I found myself learning the Bible and making some close, new friends besides. There were seven of us who came to the first meeting, and we stayed at that number for the whole first year of study. At that time we had too much growing and learning to do on an individual basis, and we were able to ask many questions and look for the answers while we remained small in number. After that the Lord increased the numbers in that group so that we had to break up and divide into more groups—and that's what it's all about! We were from all denominations, but, coming together with one purpose, it wasn't long before we came to the same conclusion: Jesus was the only way to the Father, the one true Savior. Whatever doctrinal problems existed, they disappeared one by one as we came to realize the simple message of love and mercy through the saving grace of Jesus Christ. I didn't understand it all clearly, but I was beginning to and that was progress for me.

Slowly, through the adult Sunday school at church, we were beginning to see our foolishness in accepting only parts of the Bible. We saw our pride in deciding to judge what was right and what was wrong in Scripture. Either it was all true or God was lying—either it was all the Word of God or none of it was. We saw that all our questions had answers in Scripture if we took the time to look, and we realized we had been wrong to reject any part of it.

When the phone rang one afternoon it was Solveig calling. She was a friend from church who had been helping in the Sunday school with the young people. She had word

---

[1]Neighborhood Bible Studies, Box 222, Dobbs Ferry, New York 10522.

about our older boy, Jim, who had recently come back from a weekend church retreat at a camp.

"I know how some of these young people keep things to themselves, and I knew you and Rich would want to know. Jim was one of the kids who went forward to accept Christ."

Tears of happiness flowed out as she went on. Jim had accepted Jesus the second night of the retreat—January 4, 1969. He was twelve years old, but born again into a new beginning. He hadn't said a word to us about it. I thanked Solveig for having called and thanked the Lord, too.

Jim's decision stirred a bit of conviction in my own heart. I called myself a "born-again Christian," but only in "safe" Christian circles, and I never confessed Him in any other place. Somewhere in the Scriptures I recalled mention of verbal confession and public commitment,[2] and suddenly I wasn't too sure I had really done either one. A seed was planted in my mind and God watered it with conviction in the days ahead. Praise God, He knows our hearts and has all the perfect mercy and compassion we lack. He continued to set in motion the situations that would lead me closer to Him and away from the trap that had already been set for me. Of course things got worse because God was trying to show me that there really wasn't anyone else to turn to except Him. As each new problem arose God would say to my heart, "I am the way," and my intellect would argue, "I'll just try this way first—it makes more sense." But God is a Father who demands we follow His way in faith—believing without doubt that His way is perfect, though His way is not usually man's way.

The first problem was the fact that my parents had finally separated and divorce was soon to come, leaving my mother completely alone. Then Rich's buddy from the army, his best man at our wedding, died of an untimely heart attack.

---

[2]Romans 10:9-11.

My father was living in New York City and yet wouldn't come near us because of his break with my mother. I didn't know when we would ever see him. We took a drive to Rich's family in Ohio for Christmas and the strain was unbelievable because the aunt, with whom he had been raised, was dying. Aunt Faith died a short time later and we took another trip home for the funeral. And my grandfather died soon after. It was just one thing after the other that year, and it amounted to one big tug-of-war, with our souls at stake. Which way would I decide to go? I knew I had the choice and that I had to make it immediately.

It was Easter Sunday, April 6, 1969, and as we got ready for church I decided that if the pastor gave an altar call, I would go forward. I had been fighting the idea for so long that I now realized it had to be very important. It made me uncomfortable to know that going forward was an admission to all my friends that I really hadn't been born again after all. Maybe they'll think I lied to them, I thought, and all the way to church I had a terrible battle with my feelings. But did it really matter what anyone thought? Wasn't it far more important to do what God had said in His Word? I had worried all my life about what other people thought, and now it was time I was concerned with pleasing God first. I even had a tremendous urgency about this that I had never had about anything else. I wasn't exactly sure why He wanted me to go forward, but I was sure that He expected it of me. Even though it was humiliating for me to admit that I might not have been a real Christian in His eyes before, I was surely going to be from now on.

I listened as the pastor gave the call for those to come forward to give their lives to Jesus and experience spiritual rebirth—the rebirth that God tells us in Scripture is necessary for communion with Him. We can be good church members as I was, but that isn't enough. We can go to church all our lives, but somewhere along the line God expects us to decide for ourselves whether to accept Him or reject Him. He does not force salvation on us (1 Pet. 1:18, 19, 23). The minister went on to explain that no matter how good we've been, the Bible says that we "all have sinned and come short of the glory of God" (Rom. 3:23). "The wages of sin is death; but the gift of God is eternal life *through Jesus Christ* our Lord" (Rom. 6:23). In other words, accepting Jesus' blood sacrifice for *our* sins was the only way God had provided to cover them and wipe them out of our lives, *and* out of God's remembrance ("who his own self bare our sins in his own body on the tree, that we, being dead to sins, should live unto righteousness" (1 Pet. 2:24).

"Come forward," the minister said, "and commit your lives to God through His son Jesus Christ. Accept Him as your own personal Saviour, realizing that you must be born again, as Jesus said, in order to see the Kingdom of God (John 3:3). This is a spiritual rebirth, 'not of blood, nor of the will of the flesh, nor of the will of man, but of God' (John 1:13). For, 'if any man be in Christ, he is a new creature: old things are passed away; and all things are made new' (2 Cor. 5:17). Now is the time to make things in your life new. Now is the time to ask Jesus to come into your heart."

The hymn began:

> Just as I am, without one plea
> But that Thy blood was shed for me,
> And that Thou bidd'st me come to Thee,
> O Lamb of God, I come! I come!

I fairly flew up the aisle to the front of the church. It was difficult for me to be the first one, but purposely I wanted to do the most difficult thing—it was my way of giving a sacrifice to the One who had sacrificed everything for me.

> Just as I am, tho' tossed about
> With many a conflict, many a doubt,
> Fighting and fears within, without,
> O Lamb of God, I come! I come!

When I had reached the altar, the power of God fell on me and a strong vibration surged through my whole body as if from the inside out. I thought surely I would fall from the shaking, and struggled to maintain my balance and stay on my feet. I wondered what I'd do if I fell down in front of all those people! I knew I wasn't nervous, but I couldn't understand what was happening to me. I begged God to help me stay standing and could think of nothing else until I looked up and saw a man from the choir walk out and join me. Now there were two of us up there. I had a strong desire for my own husband to be the next one to come forward.

> Just as I am, Thou wilt receive,
> Wilt welcome, pardon, cleanse, relieve;
> Because Thy promise I believe,
> O Lamb of God, I come! I come!

The song was finished and there were still just the two of us standing at the altar. The minister stepped down and stood beside the man next to me, saying a short prayer with him that I couldn't hear. I was still worrying about falling over—why didn't the minister come to me first so that I could go sit down?

Finally the pastor came to me and laid his hand gently on my shoulder. The shaking instantly stopped and the most tremendous peace flooded over me. His prayer was short and loving. I was so excited, I could hardly wait to get back to my family. I wanted to share my joy and peace with them.

From that time on, I was a different person. I didn't notice much difference in the mirror, but I was very different inside. For the first time I could understand many of the things I didn't understand at all before. It was as if I had a new mind that brought new understanding. The Bible teaches that the things of God are not learned with the mind, but are discerned spiritually and revealed by God's own Spirit only to His children (1 Cor. 2:9-14). This new mind carried over into other things too: My values changed and I found myself no longer attracted to things that had attracted me before, and vice-versa. God had begun a new work in my life and I fairly danced through each new day. Burdens were really lifted off my mind, and things which bothered me before now seemed small and unimportant. I had never been concerned about Rich's salvation before, but now I began to pray fervently that he might have this same experience.

My neighbor, Joan, called with something new. Billy Graham was coming to New York City for a big crusade in Madison Square Garden in June, and many prayer groups were being formed all over the greater New York area to pray for the success of the crusade. Would I meet with her and another neighbor for this purpose? I had never done anything like this and welcomed the chance to help in even a small way. But as the time to gather with the other women grew closer, I found myself more and more worried about how I would pray out loud in front of other people—my prayer times had always been alone. I remembered how eloquently Mrs. Jones had prayed, using "thee" and "thou," and I just wasn't used to talking like that. I thought that all public prayer had to be phrased religiously, as anyone I had ever heard prayed this way.

That morning I finally had some idea of what I was going to say when it was my turn to pray. I walked to Joan's, hoping that there wouldn't be too much conversation ahead of time so that I'd forget what I was going to say.

The radio was playing and Edna was already there. After our greetings, she explained that a program would start any minute to lead us into our prayer time. It was sponsored by the crusade people for this purpose. By the time we had heard the program, Edna had read a scripture verse, and she and Joan had both prayed, I had forgotten my prepared words! I felt a bit frantic, but I was on the spot and had to begin somewhere. I began with the first thing that came to mind: I prayed that God would intervene in my husband's life and cause him to be born again at the crusade. That was about all I managed that first time, but it was a start. The next time I wasn't so worried, and by the third time I couldn't wait to get there. We began to pray for all our families and neighbors as well as the Billy Graham Crusade. We saw mighty miracles as a result of those prayers; I could see the need—the responsibility—for Christians to gather for prayer. Somehow through a group there is added strength—added power.

The night of the crusade found us on a bus with church friends and neighbors. Because my mother had been with us the night before, she decided to take the bus into New York City with us and go home. We talked her into going to the crusade with us first.

It was a thrilling sight. The new Madison Square Garden was filled to capacity and a two-thousand-voice choir sang praises to God, the most beautiful singing I had ever heard. I was excited when Billy Graham stepped up to the microphone to give his sermon. I had never seen him in person before. I remembered how much he had already meant in my life, and was grateful. His sermon was entitled "Heaven and Hell," and I hung on every word.[3]

> Tonight Christ can help you. He can take the guilt away and He can give you a joy, a peace, and a new dimension of living if you let Him. . . I want to talk tonight about the future life and the choice we must make now.
>
> . . . Jesus says, "Enter ye in at the strait gate: for wide is the gate, and broad is the way that leadeth to destruc-

---

[3] This is the sermon that was actually given on that night of June 17, 1969. It is condensed and taken from the book entitled *The Challenge*, by Billy Graham. *The Challenge*, copyright © 1969 by Billy Graham. Quotations used by permission.

tion, and many there be which go in thereat: Because strait is the gate, and narrow is the way, which leadeth unto life, and few." Notice our Lord said "few there be that find it" (Matt. 7:13,14). Jesus Christ taught that there are two roads of life. He taught that there are two masters. You are either mastered by self or you are mastered by God, and He said you cannot serve both at the same time. And He said that there are two destinies, heaven and hell . . . life is only a preparation for eternity.

. . . Jesus said that Hell was not prepared for man. God never meant that man would ever go to Hell. Hell was prepared for the devil and his angels, but man rebelled against God and followed the devil (Adam and Eve).

. . . You have a choice—the broad road, or the narrow road. . . . The Bible teaches there is a judgment. "God will bring every deed into judgment with every secret thing whether good or evil." . . . Whatever Hell may mean, it is separation from God. . . . Hell is death to the spirit, death to the soul, separation from God.

. . . You cannot work your way to heaven and you cannot buy your way to heaven. It is a gift of God because of what Christ did on the Cross. "So by grace are ye saved, through faith, and that not of yourself. It is a gift of God, not of works lest any man should boast" (Eph. 2:8, 9).

. . . There are mysteries known only to God. There is a mystery to Hell; there is a mystery to Heaven. I personally believe that the Bible teaches that Heaven is a literal place. . . . I know it is going to be where Jesus is. The Bible says that those of us who know Christ—the moment you accept Christ, you become a citizen of Heaven. . . . You experience Heaven the moment you receive Christ.

. . . I remember a story that when Mayor LaGuardia was mayor of this city or when he was a judge, I guess, a man was brought before him during the depression. He had stolen a loaf of bread to feed his family. And the mayor had to fine him $50. Then the mayor looked at the audience in the courtroom and said, "This court is not only one of justice, it is one of mercy." And then he fined everyone in the courtroom $1 for allowing conditions to exist where a man had to steal to provide for his family.

And he gave the money to the man and said, "Pay your fine and go your way and sin no more," and that is exactly what Jesus did. He paid the fine for us. He took the hell and the judgment and the destruction and the end of that broad road for us. Now God says, "I love you. I forgive you. Go and sin no more."

You start through that narrow gate and live on the narrow road, and you are going to be in Heaven. Which road are you on tonight? Which direction are you traveling? Are you going toward destruction or are you going toward life? Which way? You can make the choice tonight. You can take the first step. Now it's costly. It's not easy to go through that narrow gate, and it's not easy to follow Christ. But it is a glorious and wonderful experience even here on this earth—the joy, the peace, the security, the sense of forgiveness, that He gives you—all this and Heaven too—by a choice that you make.

You say, "Well, why did God make it so simple?" He made it simple so everybody could enter—anybody can believe. Anybody can receive. Anybody can come by faith. He said, "Whosoever will, let him come." The offer is open to everyone here tonight. Will you come?

And the people began to get up out of their seats and walk down the stairs to stand in front of the platform where Dr. Graham stood waiting to pray with them. At first a few came, but soon many, and then there were hundreds from all over the auditorium pouring onto the floor. I was deeply touched and totally involved in watching the crowds when my friend Joan literally pounded me on the arm.

"Look, Nancy, it's Rich! He went forward!"

Tears flowed to block my view and I grabbed Joan in a vice-like grip of excitement. Here was the answer to all my recent prayers.

"Why didn't you go down, too?" my mother asked.

"But, Mom, I already did in church—last Easter Sunday. This is Rich's turn." I was too excited to ask her why she herself hadn't gone down!

We all fairly floated home on the bus that night. I think it could easily have taken us home if we had lost all four wheels and the engine! We laughed, we sang, we hugged each other. There was never so much joy and love contained in one long bus ride.

CHAPTER 6

Chairman of the Board

Our lives were certainly transformed by Jesus, and God had dredged a lot of things away with His special "housecleaning"; but there were things that remained because we deliberately hung onto them of our own free wills. I wish I could say that I was so changed that I no longer yielded to temptation and that I immediately loved everyone, and that life held no more problems, but it just wasn't so.

Our past conditioning often plays a part in how we react to present situations. As Jesus enters our hearts we learn that God's ways are not our ways, and a *re*conditioning process begins to take place by His Spirit and by our study of the Word. God works in different ways with each of us, arranging situations that reveal to us the muck and mire that is in us.

Something else had happened a few weeks before that was also changing the direction of our lives. Rich was realizing that the cost of living was higher on the East Coast, and the salary that had supported us in St. Paul was just not enough in Mt. Kisco. Rich was aware that the films he had produced were very profitable for Prentice-Hall; and he thought if he had his own company, his talents could bring that profit directly to us. (It doesn't work that easily, of course, but such is the stuff that dreams are made of!)

We decided to pray about our situation and, for the first time, together we bowed our heads before God and simply asked Him to help us.

Rich had done free-lance work for a man in St. Paul who was the head of a Catholic educational company. They supplied a variety of religious materials, from films to posters, to parochial schools and had a good reputation in their field. Rich called Norm one day after this prayer of ours, really not knowing what to say. He discovered that this company was losing business because the Catholic schools were closing, and Norm saw the possibility of saving the company by branching into the public school field. He asked Rich to send him the films he had produced for Prentice-Hall. Soon Norm called back and asked Rich to fly to St. Paul so that he and the board of directors could talk. When Rich returned, he was all excited.

"Honey, they offered to set me up in business—my own company—doing just what I'm doing now. Only, I will be the one making the money this time."

"You mean they are going to give you the money to do this? How much?"

"Can you believe—$30,000?"

"$30,000! No, I can't believe it—I can't. That's got to be God. Wait. When do you have to pay it back?"

"Never."

"Come on, Rich. No one gives someone that much money without strings attached. I don't know much about business, but I'm sure of that."

"The only condition is that I will sign the rights to the Catholic school market over to them. They will collect the money from sales there, but I collect the money from the rest of the school market—public, private, and other religious schools—and that's a *much* bigger market. They're investing the money in the hopes that it will give their company a new market in order to boost sales. I personally think it's a last-ditch attempt to keep alive, but it's more than enough to get me started. It would mean moving back to St. Paul, though. What do you say?''

I had moved back and forth from New York so many times that I felt like a yo-yo, and farewell parties were getting embarrassing because there was always the chance we'd be back again a few months later! But I could see the potential for us and thought it was worth trying. I would miss Mt. Kisco very much because of the very close friends we had made there in only a year, but I could also see that God was in this. We had prayed for direction and this was obviously God's hand leading us. We would have been wrong to ignore a door that God was opening. While we still lived in Mt. Kisco, Rich started his new company and we began preparing for our move. This was God's company and *He* was to be Chairman of the Board—Rich was only the president!

This was a dream-come-true for Rich; but another dream that had been mine since my childhood came true because of this new company. Rich asked me to write the first film script. I was thrilled. It was a film about Lincoln's assassination—part of a series on American history which later won an award from the Freedom's Foundation of Valley Forge. I was proud for both of us! Later on I wrote another one for his company. Anyway, this began a new career for me in writing.

It was all an exciting adventure. But I regretted saying good-bye to my new Christian friends—Joan, Nancy, another Joan, two Joyces and Edna who were all part of that special Bible study in the neighborhood. And there was Solveig, the pastor, and many others from church. They all had such an important part in our new Christian faith. And my mother, some relatives and old friends we were leaving, too—it wasn't an easy parting.

But we were committed and we left believing it was

God's will for us, and that made it easier.

We settled in St. Paul in a house right next door to the one we had lived in before. We thought it would be a lot easier on the boys' adjustment to be with old friends, and we liked the neighborhood and the lake we were near. It almost seemed as if we'd never been gone.

God kept His hand on His company and blessed us through financial trials and financial rewards. There were ups and downs, but the downs obviously came when we got in God's way. There were many lessons to be learned through operating God's company, but that story is Rich's to tell. I do want to say that God proved to us that when we give Him our professional as well as our spiritual lives, He can be glorified all the more.

CHAPTER 7

Ignorance of the Law Is No Excuse

To explain what happened after we moved back to St. Paul, I have to backtrack a few years and lay the ground work for this part of the story.

I was always an avid reader, and much more interested in fact than fiction in a broad range of subjects. It was shortly after we began going to church regularly that I bought my first book on the supernatural. It was written by a well-known newspaperman and dealt with the supernatural happenings in the lives of several famous people. I was fascinated by this book. I believed that God was all-powerful and capable of anything, including any kind of unusual or supernatural accomplishment. Those days there wasn't too much on the bookshelves in this field, but I bought everything I could find from then on. As the years went on, the supply became greater and greater, and I accumulated an extensive library.

When I was nine I had my fortune told, and I remember being intrigued even then with the idea of knowing the future. In later years when I was introduced to the Ouija board and visited a medium, I was sure that this was God speaking to me through these methods. No one ever told me that this was anything but God, and those who did disapprove never said why. But the books I read spoke of these powers as coming from "God," and I believed them. In church God was not spoken of as a God of power, One who used spiritual gifts such as described in Scripture; but the books I read and the mediums I met talked of "God" this way, and I was in total agreement. My God was alive. He was "the same yesterday, today, and forever," performing the same miracles He did when He walked the earth.

Mediums often gave me advice and good news, but sometimes there was bad news, too. One medium told me that Rich would soon die in an automobile accident on the way home from work. For years I lived in fear, planning ahead and waiting for this dreadful day. If Rich was even seconds late coming home, I remembered this prediction and the worry turned to fear, then panic, until he walked in the door safely home and still with us. I didn't know that God doesn't give us fear (2 Tim. 1:7), and I thought this prediction was a helpful warning to prepare for the eventuality of his death.

The Ouija board told me that my uncle had a very serious illness and that he would die from it. This was several months before his lung cancer was diagnosed, the disease which killed him some time later. But the board also spelled out lies and sometimes it joked and taunted, while at other times it seemed pious and religious. I thought I was communicating with dead people, as well as God, through this, and I felt that through death one achieved all knowledge through God, so I listened seriously to directions or advice. I did not know that the Bible is clear on the fact that when a person dies he cannot communicate from the grave (Job 14:10-12; Eccles. 9:5, 6), nor can a true prophecy from God be false.

I talked freely about my interest in the supernatural, and one of my friends in St. Paul borrowed a book about automatic writing that I had just read and was enthusiastic about. I had tried automatic writing myself but was never successful. My friend Shirley, however, was able to sit down with her pencil and paper and almost immediately receive a force that pushed her pencil along the paper at top speeds to form words and sentences. Eventually she progressed into something called automatic painting, and the brush formed some interesting pictures under the direction of the force behind the brush as well as a voice she was now receiving in her mind that told her what colors to use. What began to trouble me was that Shirley lived her days totally by the direction of this voice and the words that the pencil formed as she wrote faithfully each morning. I couldn't put my finger on what was wrong, but to me it seemed too much like *control*—control without one's own free will being able to surface. Shirley wouldn't even mow the lawn if her "guides" told her not to. While there were strong religious overtones to the writing that came forth, I began to question seriously if this was really the way God moved in the lives of His people. I knew Him to lead gently— never using force.

I became so concerned about automatic writing that I asked two different Bible-believing ministers what they thought about it.

"We don't approve of that kind of thing and God doesn't either," they both said emphatically. But that was their only comment, and what I thought was their own personal opinion. They gave me no Scripture to prove it.

I was a new Christian and hungered more than ever for God's strength and power in my life. I didn't know much about the Bible at all, so I continued to think that God was the only supernatural force in existence. I had just learned about the reality of Satan, but it never occurred to me that he had any power that was worth considering. In my ignorance I thought that if supernatural power looked good and was used for good purposes it had to be God. I had no idea that I was rushing headlong into the occult and had long since stepped over Satan's territorial line. I was seeing firsthand the warped fruits of his power—a very real force indeed.

Several months before we moved back to St. Paul in November of 1969, Shirley had become acquainted with a medium, a man of obvious feminine traits who had two close male followers with similar leanings. This man (whom I'll call Rodney) was quickly gathering a loyal following as he gave "readings"[1] and teachings on various occult subjects. I got to know him fairly well through Shirley and went two or three times to him for private readings, thinking that God was directing his words to me. I sat in on some church services he led—this was a Spiritist Church, but that word meant nothing to me then. We sang hymns, heard a sermon, and then public readings were given.

Soon Rodney had enough faithful followers, many of whom sold their homes and gave him their life's savings, so that he could buy a mansion and open a psychic study center. He had gone into a trance and his "spirit guides" had told him what building to buy, and how. In no time he and some of his contributors were ensconced in the huge mansion, mapping out their first program of studies and engaged in a full-scale publicity campaign to inform and attract the general public. The studies included such topics as Numerology and Astrology, Meditation, Automatic Writing, Reincarnation, Yoga, and ESP; and the center made use of its indoor swimming pool and spacious grounds for recreation as well as a nursery and later a study program for young people.

It was all very attractive, but one thing about Rodney bothered me even more than his lack of masculinity; and I told Shirley about it a few times. He was obviously very talented and knowledgeable—there was no doubt he knew what he was doing and had the enthusiasm to attract others to his work—but as nice as he seemed to be, he lacked

---

[1] A "reading" is a visit to a medium for the purpose of counsel and revelation of future happenings through the use of his psychic abilities. It is simply a form of fortunetelling.

warmth and love. As dedicated as he was to his work, he seemed to lack feelings for people as individuals. I never heard him say he was doing this to help anyone, although he had obviously dedicated his life to a master he served without question; this master had turned Rodney into a talking, moving puppet for his service. He, like Shirley, lived each minute by the direction of his "guides from the spirit world." They also abstained from eating meat as part of their obedience. Was this God or wasn't it?

I went to Rodney's just a couple of days before he moved into the mansion. I walked around the packing boxes and sat down where he motioned as he took a phone call upstairs. The room was quiet and I was alone for quite some time when a painting attracted my eye.

I got up to look more closely at it. It was a hauntingly beautiful oil painting of Jesus walking on the water, His arm outstretched to the apostles sitting in the boat some distance back. I was simply fascinated by the beauty of the subject. Then my eyes went down to Jesus' bare feet. I looked and looked again, hardly believing my eyes—but, yes, it was true, on the one foot that was showing, Jesus had only four toes! And the foot was turned in such a way so that *all* the toes were showing. Every detail of that painting was exact and precise. The artist, with his obvious technical ability, could not merely have made a mistake.

I sat down and got up half a dozen times, always going back to within inches of that painting to recount the toes. Each time I got the same amount: four! I determined to ask Rodney about it; but, just as amazing, it completely slipped my mind when he called me upstairs to his den.

When I got home, I shared this with Rich. The two of us tried to figure it all out when Rich suddenly picked up our dog and waved his paw in my face.

"Honey, look . . . look. What has four toes?"

"I don't know, Rich. What are you talking about?"

"Look at the dog. He has four 'toes' on his paw like a beast—a *beast*."

I could hardly swallow as the meaning hit me. The "beast" we were both thinking about was the beast in the book of Revelation also known as the Antichrist. Could these people, and everything they followed and stood for, have something to do with the Antichrist? It was as if God had shown us something special, and we both got excited about our possible revelation.

I called Shirley, who agreed to look at the painting and count the toes herself, although I didn't tell her why. She called back and told me that the painting was done by Rodney's mother, a gifted artist, and that Jesus had just the amount of toes a perfect man should have: five!

I don't know why Shirley saw five toes, but I know for sure that *I saw four,* because I went back to count and recount so many times. What I do know is that God used this experience to reveal His truth to me, and He even made me forget it when I was determined to ask Rodney. I believe that this was God's way of protecting me from dangers only He knew at that time. I get excited every time I think of His mercy toward me in this experience.

I was back in Mrs. Jones' Bible study group and was also going to another one in our new church led by Alice, a woman my age. Suddenly in both groups negative mention was made about a subject I had never before heard brought up in Christian circles: the occult. And Alice even gave a scripture to prove her point when she said there couldn't be such a thing as reincarnation (Heb. 9:27) because man died only once, just like Jesus.

The occult was beginning to be a seriously popular attraction to an American culture that had previously outlawed it, and its appeal could no longer be ignored. Even Rich began to speak to me about his increasing doubts and fear of my interest in the study center. Because of his concern I agreed to pray about it; I honestly wanted to be in God's will but needed more proof that the supernatural was wrong.

I approached Alice one day at Bible study.

"Alice, I have a lot of questions I need answering, and I don't want to take up the time at Bible study for all of them. Do you think you could please come to my house next week where we could talk more freely?"

"Well, praise the Lord," Alice answered with a big smile. "I have been led to pray for you for quite a while now, and God told me we should get together, so this is perfect. Of course I'll come."

Every day I prayed that God would protect me if I was doing something wrong and every day I asked Him to show me the right way. By now my suspicions were growing along with Rich's, but I was still looking for something definite to back them up—some real facts to prove our theories.

By the time Alice came over to answer my questions, I felt very fond of her and had come to appreciate her extensive knowledge of the Bible as she led the studies each week with such ease and obvious capabilities. This was a very fundamental church we were all going to, and several times I had considered leaving Alice's study group as the women piously discussed all the things they DIDN'T do, sometimes at great lengths. At that point I did almost everything they boasted they didn't do, having been raised to think these things perfectly innocent and normal. For a time I sat by silently listening and wondering what I was doing there, but I could see that Alice herself did not really appreciate all of this talk (though she was lovingly tolerant), and I decided to stay in the group and give it another try. If I had left the group, I might never have invited Alice over that afternoon.

After we greeted each other and chatted about the usual pleasantries, I got to the subject.

"Alice, I've asked questions of so many people who have a studied knowledge of the Bible, but I have never gotten any real answers. I feel as though somehow you're the one God wants to use to supply them to me. You said you have been praying for me, and that alone thrills me. I just feel that confirms the fact that this visit is very important."

Alice went on to tell me that God had given her some scriptures to share with me. What thrilled me so much was that this showed that God was a heavenly Father who cared about me as an individual and who knew what my question was, indicating it to Alice through Scripture before I even asked.

"I'm very concerned about my friend Shirley and the way her life is controlled by something called automatic writing. Do you know anything about this?"

Alice went on to tell me that she was well aware of it and the other things I mentioned in connection with the psychic study center, as she herself had a background in similar things before she became a Christian.

"Here," Alice continued, "let's read some of this scripture first. It might help as an introduction. I have a New American Standard Bible, but you can follow along in yours if you want to. Go to Colossians, chapter 2, verse 6, 'As you therefore have received Christ Jesus the Lord, so walk in him.' Now verse 8, 'See to it that no one takes you captive through philosophy and empty deception, according to the tradition of men, according to the elementary principles of the world, rather than according to Christ. For in him all the fulness of deity dwells in bodily form, and in him you have been made complete, and he is the head over all rule and authority.' Ask yourself, Nancy, if these things you asked about are fulfilling the command that once we have made Jesus Lord of our lives, we must 'walk in him.' Are these things glorifying men—ourselves—or Christ? You see, it says that the fullness of God himself is complete in Jesus—as are we—and Jesus must rule all the authority that we as Christians follow. Is Jesus at the center of their rules—their teachings?

"All right, now down to verse 16, 'Let no one act as your judge in regard to food or drink.' Didn't you tell me that they have all been told by their 'guides' that they must not eat meat? 2 Timothy 4:1-5 talks about this, too, and goes on to say that God has made all food for us to be eaten gratefully, blessed by the Word of God and prayer.

"Now to verse 18 in Colossians again, 'Let no one keep defrauding you of your prize by delighting in self-abasement and the worship of the angels' (and that could be fallen angels too—they are demons), 'taking his stand on visions he has seen, inflated without cause by his fleshly mind, and not holding fast to the head, from whom the entire body, being supplied and held together by the joints and ligaments, grows with a growth which is from God.' And the 'head' is Jesus. Without Him, who is our strength and nourishment, we cannot have life.

"And now to get to the point, let's turn to 2 Corinthians, chapter 11, verses 13 through 15. It warns first that many will come teaching a Christ who is different from the one whom the Scriptures teach, thereby changing God's truths. 'For such men are false apostles, deceitful workers, disguising themselves as apostles of Christ. And no wonder, for even Satan disguises himself as an angel of light. Therefore, it is not surprising if his servants also disguise themselves as servants of righteousness; whose end shall be according to their deeds.'

"And then 1 John, chapter 4, verses 1-6, tells us that everything must be tested to see whether it is from God or Satan, because it says, too, that there are many who are out to deceive us with things that seem good. Verse 2, 'By this you know the Spirit of God: every spirit that confesses that Jesus Christ has come in the flesh is from God.' Verse 3, 'And every spirit that does not confess Jesus, is not from God.'

"Part of the reason for these words of caution is that God has real gifts of the Spirit like miracles, prophecy, healing, tongues, etc.—all for the edification of the church and for power in drawing people to Jesus Christ for salvation and cleansing[2]—but Satan has counterfeits for these gifts, too,

---

[2]See 1 Corinthians, chapters 12 and 14, for more detail on the gifts of the Spirit. Also see 1 Corinthians 12:7,28; Acts 13:1; 1 Corinthians 14:3,4,5;

for the opposite purpose: to mislead and destroy.

"God warns us that these satanic powers are very real and very harmful to us, so He forbids our investigation of them *for our own good.*[3] Even the word occult means secret or hidden things. And following after a use of this forbidden power is *rebellion against God* because He has commanded against it. Even ignorance of God's laws in this area is no excuse when it comes to falling prey to Satan and the harm of stepping out of God's will here."

Alice then went on to explain that one often needs special ministry to be free from any damage in this area because of occult involvement. Sometimes the damage can range from physical illnesses to thoughts or attempts of suicide. Authoritative Christian ministry in the name of Jesus can completely free Satan's intended victim.

There wasn't one thing that Alice said that I rejected. She was speaking directly to me from the written Word of God, and I couldn't deny what that said. All of the things I had thought were from God I now knew were not. It was not easy to realize that I had been so deceived, but I knew very well that it was directly related to the fact that I didn't know the scriptural warnings.

"Well, Alice, if anyone was involved, I sure was. Do you think I need ministry, too? I don't want to leave anything out in getting rid of whatever effects there may be as the result of my mistake. I was wrong, and I want God's cleansing as well as His forgiveness."

We arranged to go for ministry a week later to a place in Minneapolis—a Full-Gospel fellowship of believers who willingly prayed for any needs. Alice then gave me a book to read called *The Challenging Counterfeit* by Raphael

---

and Ephesians 4:11-12 where it speaks of the gifts to be used for the Church of Christ in edification and to glorify Jesus.

[3]Leviticus 19:26,31; 20:27; Deuteronomy 18:10-14; Acts 16:16-20 (demonic deliverance of a fortuneteller).

Gasson (Pub., Logos), a former medium turned Christian.[4]
That book answered most of the questions I had left, and I
cancelled my class at the psychic study center and any
future plans I had there, and turned my back forever on the
entire realm of the occult. I then began many burdened
weeks of prayer for Shirley, whom I loved and couldn't
forget in my concern. I just had to wait for the right time to
talk to her but, for the time being, we lost touch with each
other. I didn't know how to tell her.

---

[4]Also good on the subject is: *Angels of Light,* by Hobart Freeman, Pub.,
Logos; *I Talked With Spirits,* by Victor H. Ernest, Pub., Tyndale House;
Like a Roaring Lion, by George Otis, Pub., Time-Light; *Sorcery in
America,* series of four, and *The Mystery of Jeane Dixon,* by Gordon Lind-
say, 50¢ each, Pub., Christ for the Nations, Box 24910, Dallas, Texas,
75224.

CHAPTER 8

By Water and the Spirit

At church they had been handing out a tiny booklet called, *Have You Made the Wonderful Discovery of Spirit-Filled Life?* by William R. Bright of Campus Crusade for Christ. It talked about how every day could by an "exciting adventure" when one was filled with God's Holy Spirit. The idea absolutely fascinated me, although one thing confused me. It said that the way to be filled with the Spirit was to accept Christ as Saviour and Lord of your life. I had already done that and knew that God had created a new spirit within me, but I didn't seem to have the "power" that this booklet talked about, and if I did, I reasoned I should certainly know about it somehow.

At Bible study that week I decided to ask Alice about it. She had been talking a lot about this Spirit-filled life, too, and I wanted to have it for myself with all the fruits, power and gifts the Bible talked about.

"Alice, you and Pastor have talked so much recently about this Spirit-filled life. Please tell me, are you Spirit-filled?"

"Yes," Alice replied.

"Well, then," I asked bluntly, "how did you know when you were?"

There was a long silence as Alice looked around the room at the group of maybe ten regular ladies who were also waiting for the answer. I wondered what was taking her so long.

"Well," she finally began, "I spoke in tongues!"

There was an embarrassed silence. This was a group of women who came from a fundamental church that never talked about such things.

"If you spoke in tongues, then you'd *know for sure* you were filled with the Spirit!" I said, trying quickly to cover the silence.

Alice went on to explain that it was the same thing that happened to the apostles and the others who waited in the upper room for what Jesus promised: a baptism with the Holy Spirit (Acts 1:5) that would give them *power* to minister and be His witnesses (Acts 1:8). Jesus said they had to have this to be effective, and they were already born-again believers who had been baptized in water! The first thing that happened after the Holy Spirit came from heaven and "filled them" was that they began to "speak with other tongues" (Acts 2:4). And this same pattern is followed closely in the rest of Scripture, with the gift of tongues following the baptism with the Holy Spirit, usually by the laying on of hands. In Acts chapter 8 the apostles sent Peter and John to Samaria to pray specifically for those who had received the gospel of Jesus and had been baptized in water, so they might *then* receive the Holy Spirit through prayer and the "laying on of hands" (verses 15-17). It was, therefore, considered an act important enough to send two men from Jerusalem to Samaria, a long trip in those days of over forty miles.

The Bible study ended the discussion that barely got started. Alice came up to me later to confirm our plans for the ministry I was to have at a charismatic fellowship in Minneapolis.

"Will Tuesday night be okay, Nancy?" Alice asked.

"And is it all right if Grace comes? She says she wants prayer, too."

The plans were fine and Grace was a mutual friend, the first person I had met in our new church, so I was pleased to have her along. She had never been to one of these meetings either, and I was glad for her support as Rich had already said he didn't want to go.

When Alice, Grace, and I drove into Minneapolis that frigid Tuesday evening in November, 1969, I wondered if I'd ever get used to the Minnesota winters with snow and ice and constant cold for months on end. Once the car heater got going it was easier to relax and think about the meeting ahead. I was especially excited about the possibility of facing problems or meeting needs with prayer rather than having to go to a psychiatrist, as had been my pattern for so many years. I knew God had answers man didn't have.

My only big apprehension involved an article I had seen several years ago about a religious meeting, complete with photos of people lying on the floor, jumping all over the room, and obviously shouting out loud when they felt so inclined. I was relieved to get an aisle seat when we arrived, as I fully intended to run out if the activities got as wild! To keep check on this possibility, I spent the entire meeting with my eyes wide open and head scanning the room so that if anyone started acting "crazy," I wouldn't lose a second finding out!

The meeting began with a time of singing songs, most of which, Alice explained, were verses from Scripture set to music. As people sang and worshipped they occasionally lifted their hands in the air as if reaching out to Jesus himself, just like in the words of the Psalm we had been singing, "I will lift up my hands in thy name" (Ps. 63:4). I never saw such ecstasy as those people had on their faces—why, they literally glowed!

A prayer time led into something I had never heard before, but knew what it must have been almost as soon as it began: singing in tongues. I had never heard anything so exquisitely beautiful in all my life! I was entranced and imagined that the angels in heaven must sound like this when singing praises to God around His throne.

Then a woman from the congregation got up to say that she felt God was speaking to her heart about the trials someone there was going through now, and that they should be assured that God was using these things to mold and strengthen them like a potter at a wheel does with a piece of clay.

Others rose to tell of healings or blessings, each time thanking Jesus and giving Him the glory.

Then it was time for the sermon. The minister had been sitting with the elders and had taken the lead in most of the service. He was a warm man with an eager smile and relaxed manner and the words simply flowed from his mouth as he spoke without notes. I was surprised to hear him speak on the same subject Rodney had talked about a few weeks before: the vital importance of love—only Rodney didn't have love, whereas this man seemed to glow with it! What a difference! I felt God was showing me the truth in this very real and special way.

The meeting ended with everyone going downstairs for coffee and an invitation for those who wanted prayer to come upstairs later. The minister and some of the elders were waiting when we came back upstairs, and we seemed to be the only ones. Alice introduced us and I began to explain what I was there for.

"I was involved in the occult, thinking it was God's work. As soon as I found out it wasn't, because of my husband's concern and through Alice's help, I broke all contacts. I realize from what Alice said that I need prayer now to completely break any spiritual ties that remain. Also, I think I should mention that I had a problem with suicide attempts way back, and have had to battle urges in that direction as recently as last year."

The minister and the elders listened patiently and then

agreed to pray for me. I can't remember the words, but they all laid hands on my head or shoulders and that was the first time I had ever had that kind of personal ministry. It was very beautiful. They took authority in the name of Jesus over any forces of the enemy in these areas and I recall the minister having me verbally renounce these things myself.

When it seemed to be over, the minister asked, "Would you like us to pray for you to receive the baptism with the Holy Spirit now?"

It was a question that caught me totally unprepared, but I agreed.

They told me to lift my hands to the Lord while they prayed for me. It was a gesture I wasn't used to and my arms quickly tired. The prayer seemed short enough, but they waited and waited. My arms were still in the air, and they began to hurt because of this difficult position; I could think of almost nothing else. Suddenly I realized that they were waiting for me to "speak in tongues"! I was horrified. I couldn't talk like that in front of all these people and, even if I wanted to, I wouldn't have known how to begin! No words came to my mind—I didn't know what to do. Finally the minister decided to let Alice continue praying with me alone. They were all so loving and patient that by this time I was feeling frustrated and guilty that nothing happened—all this on top of the pain in my arms!

Alice assured me that the Lord said I was baptized with the Spirit for sure and that I could now speak in tongues. She quoted Luke 11:13 where it says that God will always give the Holy Spirit to those who ask, and hadn't I asked? I tried to please everyone—uppermost in my mind was the fact that I would really make *them* happy if I spoke in tongues—but I had totally lost sight of the fact that I should *first* be anxious to obey and please *God*. I was still embarrassed, and I didn't really understand why I had to speak in tongues anyway. I wanted the baptism, all right, but I frankly didn't want to speak in tongues! Especially not in front of all those people!

Finally Alice stopped praying with me and told me not to worry about it anymore. We then turned our attention to Grace, who all this time had been waiting for her prayer ministry.

I really felt happy on the way home, and my arms were feeling so much better too. It was all so new to me I was in a daze. Grace had been prayed for and hadn't received her "tongues" yet either—the same arguments and fears had run through her mind. We were both relieved that the pressure was off us. We thanked Alice as we said goodnight, and I didn't think much more about it all until Grace called a few days later.

"Nancy, I have my complete baptism now. I'm really filled with the Spirit—tongues and everything. I can't tell you what an experience it was."

I begged her to tell me how it had all come about. I knew that Grace was battling the idea of speaking in tongues even more than I was, because she had a painful shyness to overcome that was much stronger than my embarrassment; and, she, too, had argued that "tongues" were unnecessary. She said she had read a very good book that helped her understand it better, and it so inspired her that she asked for the baptism by herself at home and received it right away. I never heard her so excited about anything before.

Grace offered to go with me to a Christian bookstore to help me find this book, and when we got there I could see why. It must have been a book they had by accident, as the store carried no other books on the subject and it was buried under several other books on a bottom shelf in the very back of the store. Today, five years later, that same store proudly features charismatic books by the dozens. The demand is now so great and the ten bestselling Christian books are now mostly charismatic.

The book, *Face Up With a Miracle* by Don Basham, proved truly absorbing. I couldn't put it down. It was the story of Don Basham and his wife who found the born-again experience as a result of seeing a friend miraculously healed on the eve of surgery. Knowing that Jesus was very real, not just yesterday but today too (Heb. 13:8), they visited the Pentecostal Christians who prayed for their friend and discovered the baptism with the Holy Spirit. Don saw the need to follow God's leading for his life, so he left his profession of commercial art to go into the ministry. While his fellow seminary students defended their complex theological theories, Don found himself defending the basic Word of God just as Scripture relates it having happened. With this simple faith, Don began to see miracles in his life that could not be explained away as mere coincidence. God was meeting the faith of this man as His Word promises. I was thrilled, because I had always believed God to be a God of love and power who wanted to heal and meet His children's everyday needs. Don's God wasn't just a Sunday God either!

I finished the book one evening in bed. Having just read Rev. Basham's chapter on how to receive the Holy Spirit baptism, I put the book down and turned to look at Rich sleeping beside me. I knew more than ever that this was the experience I wanted and now I was ready to accept it on God's terms—my arguments and intellectual reasonings were no longer important. I had a hunger for more of God—for the promise of Jesus that would fulfill in my life every need and every strength to become a powerful witness for Him. This was what He had suffered and died for—that I might be "complete in him." I wished that Rich could share all of this with me, but it was something he didn't then understand and for which he seemed to have no desire. I quietly got out of bed, trying not to disturb him, and went into the bathroom.

I got down on my knees and asked God for forgiveness. I felt so ashamed that I had rejected a part of the baptism experience—a part that He deemed important enough to bestow and then to mention over and over in His word as being edifying and even vital. I told Him that I hoped He would forgive me, and that I was now ready for His *complete* baptism, *including* the gift of tongues. I raised my hands to heaven in an automatic gesture of love and surrender and instantly I was filled with a peace and joy I had never before experienced. It was as if my whole being was lifted out of heaviness—my spirit and my soul were soaring in heavenly elation, and I felt I couldn't contain my praises to God a second longer.

I opened my mouth to speak words of love to my Father, but I heard myself singing, not speaking, and in a language I didn't know. The words just flowed forth, sounding much like Latin, and I noticed that when seeming sentences had ended, they rhymed with the end of the one before. It was like beautiful, melodic poetry! And the tune was incredibly lovely in its simplicity. I had never heard my voice so perfect in its pitch, and I sang each note as a precious offering to my Lord, my Saviour, my Baptizer—it was as if my entire self, both inside and out, was being dedicated anew into His service. My emotions were totally and completely wrapped in a new reverence and praise. My spirit was in communion with God's Spirit, and I was experiencing His perfect peace and elation in this new union with Him.

*   *   *

A few days later my mother came from New York for a month's visit over the Christmas holidays, and this, more than anything else, proved the reality of the change that had taken place within me. I had never been able to be with my mother for more than a day or two before our personalities would clash. We would be involved in such heated differences that our boys had begged me each time a visit was impending "not to fight with Grandma." As much as I wanted to love and be loved by my mother, the years had only driven us farther and farther apart. Nothing we could do for each other seemed to be enough, and underlying tensions sometimes surfaced into bitter verbal brawls.

This time our visit was different, and when my mother left a month later, Rich said, "I've never seen you get along so well with your mother, honey. Nothing she said seemed to bother you this time. You've really changed."

As a matter of fact, nothing seemed to bother me at all. I was sailing on a new high and enjoying every minute of it. I had never been so relaxed and happy.

Alice introduced me to a charismatic church near home, much closer than the one we went to in Minneapolis where I had received prayer, and I began to go there for regular "feeding" in between our usual church meetings Sunday mornings. Pretty soon I felt an urgency for the rest of the family to go to this charismatic church and though Rich was rather uncomfortable with the idea, he agreed and we began to call it our church home. There was no doubt in my mind that this was a move that God was directing. We were now in an atmosphere where the Holy Spirit was allowed to have full freedom during the services and the gifts of the Spirit were in operation. This was a small fellowship and its members were closely knit and functioning in love and concern for one another. There were very few needs that were not recognized and taken care of. It was a beautiful way to learn and grow, fully supported by the believers. The minister would stand before the congregation and say, "Just worship as the Spirit leads," and I'd think about how that should apply in our lives as well as in the service. I wanted the kind of life that was totally led by the Spirit of God.

A new burden seemed to take hold of my thoughts and I mentioned it to Rich one day.

"Honey, I can't seem to get Shirley out of my mind. All of a sudden I have a tremendous urge to pray for her.

"Nancy, I really feel she knows what she's into with that automatic writing and study center. She's not stupid."

"But, Rich, I know she loves God, I just know it. I really think she doesn't realize that she's playing with fire. My problem is that I don't know how to tell her. She's so stubborn. Once she told me that when she makes up her mind, nothing can change it."

Many times each day I brought Shirley before the Lord in prayer. Each time I thought about her it was as if I was weighted down with her burden and only as I prayed for her would I get release for a while. I told the Lord that I wanted to talk to Shirley, but He'd have to tell me when and how. There was just no way I could do it without His help.

Then, about two weeks after this burden began, I woke up one morning with an urgency to call Shirley. I tried to brush it off because I still didn't know what to say, but the thought wouldn't be ignored. To get some peace, I dialed her number. I prayed for direction as the phone rang. It had been many weeks since we had spoken to each other.

After the usual preliminary chit chat, Shirley asked what I had been doing lately. I told her about Alice's Bible study group and the new church we had been going to. I invited her to both when she sounded interested in the healings and gifts of the Spirit in operation. I didn't know it then, but Shirley had already become suspicious of the psychic study center when she had come to realize that the leaders there seemed to place far more importance on self than on God. She told the Lord that she was going into a self-imposed "retreat" at home and that she wasn't going anywhere or seeing anyone until He provided the answers to her unrest. I was her first phone call in three days. She thought I was still involved in occult things and, at first was hesitant, but she decided to take my call as a sign from God and began to go to Alice's Bible study as well as cautiously visit our new church.

It took Shirley a while to completely accept the fact that Satan had been her master when she truly thought she was following God. It was a blow to her pride and it was very difficult at first for her to understand the scriptures that explained these things. The occult teaching twisted the Bible verses to its own ends, and Shirley went through a painful state of confusion. But God had His perfect way, and with a born-again experience and the baptism with the Holy Spirit, Shirley gained strength slowly as Jesus lifted each burden and broke each shackle. God had graciously allowed me to be an instrument to this end, correcting the wrong I felt I had done in involving her with the occult in the first place. God was certainly merciful!

*   *   *

God had been talking to me for a long time about being baptized in water. I had almost gone through with it at Hillside Church when we lived in Mt. Kisco right after I was born again, but I had backed out near the last minute. I didn't really understand water baptism and, frankly, I was again worried about my public appearance, having no desire to look as unpresentable as one would coming out of all that water fully clothed. Pride and intellect were blocking the way.

Now our new minister was saying that the church was to have its first baptismal service in a lake. The idea of being baptized the way Jesus had been appealed to me more than I could resist. Suddenly it didn't matter if I didn't really understand why, just as long as I was in obedience to God's will. I made arrangements to be part of that first group and openly desired Rich to be with me in this experience. He wouldn't hear of it. Also dampening my joy, my mother, who was staying with us at the time, wouldn't even come to the service. "You were baptized as a baby, and as far as I'm concerned that's good enough," my mother flatly declared.

The baptism was scheduled for an early Sunday morning before church. Even in August the early mornings were a bit cool and the water had a chill that did not entice. I clustered with the group that pressed in close to the minister for instruction on baptism. I couldn't get my mind off my disappointments: my mother wasn't there and Rich wouldn't join me. He was hovering on the farthest edge of

94

the crowd just as if to make sure no one would push him in
by mistake. Poor Rich. He had struggled so with each painful step toward God. Why was it all so hard for him?

Suddenly God broke into my thoughts with a clear admonition to listen to the teaching and to leave Rich to Him.
I turned all my thoughts, in obedience, to the minister's
words.

"Jesus commanded those who heard and believed the
Gospel to be baptized. As it says in Matthew 28:19, where
Jesus is instructing the eleven disciples, 'Go ye therefore,
and teach all nations, baptizing them in the name of the
Father, and of the Son, and of the Holy Ghost.' The Apostle
Peter says in Acts 2:38 to 'repent, and be baptized every
one of you in the name of Jesus Christ for the remission of
sins.' When Ananias baptized Paul he told him, in Acts
22:16, to 'be baptized, and wash away thy sins, calling on
the name of the Lord.' So we see that baptism is a means by
which forgiveness and the washing away of sins is ap-
propriated. Through Christian baptism, the believer is
brought into complete union with Christ. Colossians 2:11-
12 speaks of baptism as the way into Christ's death. The
sinful man is put to death and buried with Him and finally
a new man, free from all the claims of the law of sin and
death, comes forth with Jesus in His resurrection. So baptism
is a visible means through which to appropriate an invisible
promise of grace. God has given several aids to faith such
as Communion (or the Lord's Supper), the anointing with
oil and the laying on of hands, as well as water baptism. God
intends baptism to be more than an empty sign. He promises in baptism to put us into Christ, forgive our sins and
give us the Holy Spirit, bury our old sinful selves and
raise us to new life with Christ[1]—a tangible means through
which we can be united with Him. Praise God, it's a wonderful and holy experience."

[1]Galatians 3:26, 27; Acts 2:38; Acts 22:16; Romans 6:3-5.

We all followed the minister and I felt a nudge as I got near the water. It was Alice.

"Get up there, Nancy, and be the first one to be baptized."

She gave a shove and the minister held out his hand. I was the first one. He asked me to give a testimony and said that everyone should be prepared to say a few words as they came in the water.

"Dear God, I'm sorry I didn't get baptized before. Forgive me for waiting so long." And down I went, backwards, as the minister held me across the back of the shoulders. And out of the water I came praising God and knowing that, in faith, I had obeyed His Word.

> For they heard them speak with tongues, and magnify God. Then answered Peter, Can any man forbid water, that these should not be baptized, which have received the Holy Ghost as well as we? And he commanded them to be baptized in the name of the Lord . . ."
>
> Acts 10:46-48

I came on the shore, greeted with the hugs and tears of my friends as they wrapped a towel around me. I looked to the back of the crowd where Rich stood motionless and unsmiling. I walked to him, so anxious to share my joy with him too. I couldn't keep still. As I put my wet arms around him I heard myself say, "Honey, it isn't too late for you."

He didn't say a word as he looked toward the lake. The last person had just been baptized and the minister was still in the water. Rich handed me the camera he was holding, took off his watch and gave me that too, kicked off his shoes, and went out in the lake. Tears splashed down my cheeks as I remembered God's earlier admonition to leave Rich to Him. Praise the Lord! He had been dealing with Rich in his heart all along. Only God can see into the heart of a man; I never could have known by Rich's outward actions that he would walk into the lake that day.

As he came out from the water I embraced Rich tightly. "Honey, the Bible says the last shall be first and the first shall be last. That's really both of us today. Isn't it exciting?"

Dripping wet, clothes hanging limply, we both smiled as our friends gathered around us. I looked up and saw my mother walking toward us, but she had missed everything.

*   *   *

God means for the husband to be the spiritual head of the household, a loving, Christlike representative of God himself for the wife and children.[2] For spiritual safety and comfort, this is the order that God has declared to be perfect. When the balance is off, the whole family is affected adversely. Part of the desire that God put in my heart as a loving wife was to see my husband have everything that God had for him. I didn't know much about spiritual order at that time, but I wanted to be able to look up to my husband as a trusted decision maker—someone who knew what God wanted for us as a family. I was not comfortable making decisions for the children and myself that I often felt forced to make. I needed help and direction without having to run to the church—the pastor and the elders—all the time, and the children needed this, too. So I began to pray for my husband more than ever and this time I asked God to baptize Rich with His Holy Spirit just as He had baptized me. I wanted this for the children too. If I needed the power and strength of the Holy Spirit, certainly my husband and children needed it just as much.

I asked friends to pray, too, and those who saw Rich frequently were a great personal comfort to me with their encouragement. They could see that Rich was uncomfortable in church and around Christian fellowship. They prayed

---

[2]Ephesians 5:22-33.

with me that God would move in his life to draw Rich closer to Him. I longed for the day when Rich would be by my side in spirit as well as body, enjoying the fullness of life in Jesus without any hindrances, sharing with me the excitement of life lived by the leading of God's Spirit. There is just nothing that compares with it.

I had seen in others the result of nagging, so realized that a verbal onslaught would drive Rich farther and farther away. Most of the time I looked to God for leading in what to do or say to Rich when it came to spiritual matters, and, praise the Lord, He also gave me strength and encouragement through many trying situations. God assured my heart that this problem or that problem would work out, and He gave me added grace as I needed it. Without my even knowing it, God was placing in my heart the desire to follow the scriptural admonition to be quiet and patient.[3] It is a loving, sympathetic, compassionate manner that draws one nearer to the things of God. And this is never by our own efforts, but by allowing Christ to live and work in us.

There were times that I would tire and lose patience, and there were times when I would become angry and despair; but Jesus always led me back to the right track and Rich couldn't help but notice. Even though he was uncomfortable at church, he went to please me, and he knew it was good for the boys. He saw the change in me and knew the Spirit-filled life was right even though something in him rebelled against it for himself. The forces of good and evil worked a tremendous battle in his soul. One day he said to me that this spiritual warfare and the Korean War were the two hardest conflicts in his whole life. I was horrified. My poor husband needed help and I wasn't sure what to do.

Our dear Lord is always anxious for us to turn our problems to His care. When we do, He *always* provides the answer. This was no exception. He told me to go and have

---

[3] 1 Peter 3:1-9.

the church pray with me for Rich.

Our church was small enough then to provide this opportunity. During the testimony time there was a chance to ask for help and the minister led the whole church in prayer for Rich. He concluded by asking God to lead him to the baptism with the Holy Spirit. The very next day Rich said he was ready to go for prayer for the baptism! It was all I could do to keep myself from telling him about the prayer of the congregation the night before, but somehow I knew it wasn't the time yet. Rich said he had decided to go to the same church in Minneapolis where I had received my baptism, so I called Shirley and asked her if she would come with us—we had gone through so much together and I wanted her to be a part of it.

I was so excited as we got ready to go into Minneapolis to church that night, I almost danced on the ceiling. After all, I had waited a long time for this very special occasion! The drive to church seemed twice as long as usual, and I had an awful time keeping my mind on the service. When it was finally over the pastor announced the special prayer time after the coffee break, and Rich turned to Shirley and me.

"I'm not going to stay for prayer after all. Let's go."

"What? What are you saying, honey? I thought we came all this way especially for prayer." I practically burst into tears. What did this sudden reversal mean?

Rich went on to explain that since the regular minister wasn't there, he "didn't like the looks" of the one who had replaced him, so he decided that he wasn't going to let this new one pray for him! Even now it's hard for me to describe my disappointment because it was so intense. I don't remember actually crying, but I know that it was all I could do to keep from doing so. Poor Shirley tried to be a comfort, but what could she really do or say? She was as dumbfounded as I was. All we could do was go home and keep on praying.

A couple of nights later nothing seemed to have changed, so I sought God alone again to ask what I could do to help

Rich. I had an impression that I should pray against Satan's attempt to prevent Rich from coming into God's fullness, so I did this out loud and with the confidence that it was directed from God. I commanded Satan to take his hands off Rich so that he could be free to receive the baptism. Then I thanked God for His help and for the blood that Jesus shed to make this victory possible.

That night I was leafing through a new book entitled *Faith* by Hobart Freeman. I hadn't read it yet, but I felt a strong impulse to give it to Rich. This I did in faith because I knew that Rich didn't like to read. He surprised me by taking the book and reading all thirty-seven pages that evening. The book gives excellent instructions on how to receive the baptism with the Holy Spirit. I have since passed this book on to many people who have received the baptism as a result of following the instructions. Rich later told me that this book helped him in the same way.

Rich didn't say much about the book, but the next day he said he was ready for prayer again; this time he was going to go to our own church and have our own minister pray for him. The time to do this was at the special prayer session on Sunday night after the regular service, just like at the church in Minneapolis.

Again I waited with expectation through a whole service and then through what seemed like an endless coffee time. I heard the minister say he thought there wasn't anyone who wanted prayer that night. I almost panicked because I was afraid Rich would not say anything to him about it. One of our friends was next to me and I told him to please tell the minister that Rich wanted prayer and that this was too important to put off. It had been almost two weeks since we were at the church in Minneapolis, and I didn't want to wait another minute longer. (We wives can be so impatient for our husbands!)

Some of us went upstairs, and this time I had a lot of friends to share the moment with me. These were people to

whom I felt very close in the Lord—people who had been
such an encouragement and comfort to me. They all had
prayed for Rich to receive this added power in his life, and
it seemed right that they should now see their prayers
fulfilled.

I sat clutching Shirley's hand as Rich stood for prayer in
the front of the church, the elders and deacons around him.
He told them that he was there to receive the baptism with
the Holy Spirit, and the minister laid hands on him and
began to pray.

I squeezed Shirley's hand even harder and tears of joy
rolled down my face and fell into my lap. I had known God
was going to bring Rich to this place, but I could hardly
grasp the reality of it.

I couldn't hear what was being said, but the next thing I
knew Rich was speaking out loud and clearly in tongues,
and everyone around him was rejoicing and praising the
Lord.

"I don't believe it. I don't believe it." My mouth was
seemingly incapable of voicing any other words. And I must
have cried a lake in my tremendous happiness and excitement. I had never before seen a baptism happen so easily
and freely (though I know it happens all the time), and the
visions and words of prophecy that came forth next made it
one of the most unusual and thrilling baptisms I have seen
to this day. God was blessing His son with His precious, free
gift of the Holy Spirit according to His Word; and He was
blessing me, His daughter, by allowing me to share in the
experience though Rich hadn't been able to share mine.
God built us both up that night and began a holy work that
made us truly "one in the Spirit."

Being baptized with the Holy Spirit is not an end in
itself. It is just the beginning. It is through this process that
God can live in your life and spirit as you have never
dreamed possible. It is opening a door to the power and
glory of God to flow through every fiber of your being—all
so that Jesus can be lifted up and glorified. He can then

draw all who will come to His precious well to drink freely of His peace, His healing touch, and His love.

That night, almost one year after Jesus baptized me with His Holy Spirit, God filled Rich to overflowing. Together Rich and I felt this healing in our souls, the peace that passes all understanding, and the true love that comes only from Jesus.

CHAPTER 9

Dying to Self and Learning How to Step Over the Body Gracefully

There is nothing like a baby on the way to change a person's life and teach many valuable lessons in the process! Our two boys were to be ten and fifteen years old when the baby was due to arrive in August of 1971. A lot of time had passed since we had a little one around the house, but Rich and I thought we'd better not wait until we were any older to have the third one we'd really wanted for so long. With genuine joy we both received the doctor's confirmation of my pregnancy, and we anticipated the fun of telling the family.

Even though we were in a rough financial position at the time, with Rich's new business in an early stage of struggle, we thought that the best way to break the news of the coming baby to the family was to take them to dinner at everyone's favorite restaurant. My mother was staying with us then, so it was perfect that she could share this, too. We made our plans and announced that we had a wonderful surprise for everyone and that it would be revealed at the dinner table. I'll never forget the scene. My mother and the two boys were nervously eyeing Rich and me, almost afraid to guess our latest "surprise." When we broke the happy news the reaction was immediate.

Jim, aged fourteen, said, "What did you have to do that to me for?"

Craig, aged nine, burst into tears and said, "What do we need with one of those?"

And my mother said, "I knew it. But you're too old and you can't afford it."

Our balloon was burst and we quickly fell down to reality with a thud. It had never occurred to us that everyone wouldn't be every bit as thrilled as we were.

God began to use the physiological changes of pregnancy to reveal many emotional weaknesses that had been held in check before. There were things God wanted to deal with that I had chosen not to face, or really thought no longer existed. One of the things was the poor relationship with my mother. There were attitudes and feelings that God knew I had to deal with before there could be a change in our relationship. The previous calm and patience I had with Mom after my baptism came to an abrupt end with a horrible confrontation over money. So often money can be a point of weakness and fear. This was the case when much of my mother's money had been tied up in a bad stock transaction—most of her savings on which she depended for her recent retirement. My frustration in the matter was based on the fact that our income had frighteningly declined that year, and I couldn't offer her any more comfort than room and board in our home. At any rate, we both had a lot of tensions and frustrations surface in that fight, and my mother left our house a short time later, vowing never to return. I was pregnant and could have used physical help as well as emotional support. The resentment and anger I felt toward my mother, as well as guilt and remorse at this new break in our relationship, were almost too awful for me to live with. I suffered terribly for months, not knowing how to rid myself of these painful feelings. I sought counsel, but to no avail.

Several months after this break with my mother, I had some free time and I asked God what He wanted me to do with it. I was really surprised when God said He wanted me to go to a movie! I couldn't believe that was He telling me that. I drove to the theater and, not having heard about either picture, I asked the cashier which picture she would recommend. (It was a double theater with one box office.) She said she had seen one of the two several times because it was so good, and directed me toward that theater. Reluctantly I paid her and found a seat just as the picture was starting.

God is so perfect in His ways and timing. He knew just what would be helpful in teaching me an important lesson. As that movie unfolded before me, I knew just exactly why He had wanted me there. It was the story of an elderly widower, recently retired, who left his home several states away to move in with his son, daughter-in-law, and grandchild in California. Already the parallel with my mother was striking. She had left her apartment-home of many years in New York City and, on her retirement, had moved in with us for several months before this break.

The man in the movie wanted to babysit with the grandchild, do the yard work, and otherwise be a help rather than a hindrance, but everything he did seemed to go awkwardly wrong—again so much like my mother's experiences. I realized that as things had gone wrong, Rich and I had reacted the way the parents in the movie reacted toward Grandpa—they took away his responsibilities one by one and pretty soon he felt useless and unwanted.

Although my mother's reactions weren't the same, God was showing me in a very clear and unmistakable way that her feelings and fears and frustrations were the same as Grandpa's in the movie. Because *I* was wrong in adding to them, I had to apologize to her no matter how wrong *she* had been in her attitudes and reactions. God was saying, "No matter how wrong the other person is, nothing justifies *your* wrong actions or *your* wrong attitudes." That movie showed me that whether or not my mother ever apologized to me or forgave me or understood my side of things, *my* attitudes and actions of forgiveness and repentance, *not* my mother's, were my responsibility before God.

When I got home from the movie, I sat down and wrote my mother a long letter telling her how wrong I had been. I didn't justify my position, I didn't ask for pity, I only asked her to forgive me. For months I had written weekly, even though she never answered my letters, because I felt it was the right thing to do. But it wasn't until I wrote this letter of repentance that *her attitude changed* and she answered back for the first time in months. This opened up a whole new line of communication between us that began a slow healing of our relationship.

God showed me that love doesn't demand anything—it doesn't expect anything—it just gives unselfishly. When I began to search my heart because of the tremendous pain that had surfaced between my mother and me, when I was willing to face the fact that I could be wrong, then God was able to move with healing. I have since learned that usually if I have a hurt, God wants to get my attention and heal a wrong action or attitude. If I don't turn away from the lesson involved, and I keep a teachable spirit, there is so much to be learned.

There has been much sadness in my life because of the inability of my parents and me to relate to each other. This parent-to-child pattern of failure and defeat can run from generation to generation, the same mistakes being made over and over. (We do tend to make the same mistakes our parents made even though we vow sternly to be "different.") But Jesus Christ suffered and died that this chain that Satan uses to keep us in bondage through the generations might be broken once and for all. The Word is full of the promises in Christ Jesus that can be fulfilled if our attitude toward our parents is right before God. "Honor your father and your mother; . . . that it may be well with you, and that you may live long on the earth" (Eph. 6:2,3). And there are many more, but *we must take action on them.*

There is much bitterness today about family environment, but I have learned that God placed me in just the home He wanted me, and with just the parents He thought I needed, for His purpose in my life. He points out over and over the purposes which have been served through each trial and heartache, and it's then that I can honestly say thank you to God for every anguish, tension and difficulty. It's then that I can feel compassion and true love for my parents despite our difficulties.

I also see now that God can speak in wisdom through my parents, and I shouldn't feel that now that I'm an adult, I don't have to listen to their advice. Certainly, my decisions are mine in the long run; but if I'm open to suggestions and tolerant of their views, God can use them with their added experiences to help and counsel me. My old attitude of rebellion toward my parents was most displeasing to God, and I could have avoided a lot of heartache if I had faced this a long time ago. Now I know that God is in control and I no longer run from the problems as they come up between us.

God wants a people who walk toward the perfection of Jesus Christ, so filled with Him that they are compelling, glowing examples of the Christian walk—a living testimony of the faith. I once heard someone say that we Christians are the only examples of Jesus some people ever see. That is a rather awesome thought.

God was using this time during my pregnancy to open my eyes to this need in my own life. I began to see the reality of Christ's admonition to take up my cross daily and follow Him, and the vital importance of allowing God to purge me of everything in my life that was standing between us. The attitudes and actions that I had been holding onto out of habit or self-indulgence had to be nailed to that cross and left there for death with Christ. I came to realize that God wanted me totally committed in every area of my life and mind.

The year the baby was born I was in the hospital five times for various reasons. Other things would have needed medical attention if God hadn't intervened with His healing touch. I was so blind to many things in my life that should have been nailed to that cross that God couldn't seem to get my attention any other way. With each new illness, each new pain or problem, I was forced to turn to God, and many times I cried out to Him to show me what He wanted. He showed me that I had to die to my own self-desires that they might be supplanted with His perfect will for me. He wanted a daily denial and death-to-self. I began to ask God to empty me of self that He might fill me with more of Him. Galatians 2:20 came alive—a declaration that I wanted true to myself.

As various issues were brought to mind by God, I often wept from the pain and humiliation of conviction. Once, like a spoiled child, I cried out, "Are you satisfied? Here I am with all my insides hanging out" (for my shame was like an exposed nakedness).

And my heavenly Father, in such wisdom, answered, "But you asked to be emptied, didn't you?"

I already stated some of the attitudes that had to change toward my parents, my mother in particular. And the same proved true in my relationship with my husband. God revealed many resentments I had toward him that I was shocked to find even existed. One of these resentments had caused me a weight problem for the first time in my life at age twenty-nine, when I gained fifty pounds in one year. For years after that I never lost weight and had even gained a few more pounds with the baby's arrival.

That year after the baby was born I attended a large annual charismatic conference in Minneapolis. The friend with whom I went was also overweight and asked one afternoon if we could stay for her to get ministry for this. I readily agreed since I hoped to take advantage of any counselling she might get. God does not want Christians to be fat. It's harmful to their health.

When the time for prayer came, I stood by her side. There

was a small group of us in a special workshop conducted by a pastor from Austin, Minnesota. When he finished teaching he called for a time of prayer. It was then that needs were expressed and the Holy Spirit poured out one of the most powerful waves of conviction and repentance I have ever seen. The pastor heard my friend's request for prayer for her weight, and I hung on every word as best I could, taking her counsel for myself.

"Gluttony is the result of not trusting God and somewhere in your life not doing His will. It is usually the effect of guilt feelings, with self-punishment by eating yourself into ill health being an unconscious result. Guilt feelings are sin because they are destructive. God wants us to ask Him to reveal to us the real problem here. You see, gluttony is not the problem. It is the result of the problem."

He mentioned that her problem might be resentment against her mother and her husband, and that she must renounce these feelings as sin before God in order to be set free from her insatiable desire to overeat.

I thought back, relating this to my life, and recalled the time I had begun to gain weight. It was in 1965 during the first move from New York to St. Paul. I could clearly see the bitterness I felt towards my husband because of my loneliness and sorrow at having to leave my family and friends. While my friend prayed for herself, I prayed quietly for myself and asked God to forgive me and set me free from this craving to eat even after a full meal.

My friend, however, couldn't then really face her problems with her mother and husband, and she continued to gain weight. But, to the glory of God, from that night on my appetite changed markedly. Without dieting, I began to lose weight slowly and safely. As I went from a size 14 dress back down to a size 10 dress, my friends and family couldn't help but notice, and that deliverance became a more impressive testimony than any other miracle I've experienced to the grace and power of Jesus.

Another issue I had to face was the fact that I tried to dominate my husband in many ways. God never intended for one person to dominate another. In my insecurity, I subconsciously reasoned that controlling a situation or a person would be a protection of sorts. Of course just the opposite is true. In interfering with God's divine order, I was actually losing my protection. When I faced this fact in our marriage relationship, Rich began to assume the responsibility he had neglected. I had been carrying burdens God never meant for me to have. When I gave them up, as God pointed them out to me, it meant a new joy for both Rich and me. He had given up assuming certain duties because I grabbed at them first. We knew we were out of order, and the whole mess resulted in guilt and condemnation for both of us. What a difference there is now as we work in unity in our proper order.

Self-pity was something else I had to deal with, for it had opened the door to depression and suicide too many times. When I confessed the entertainment of these things as sin and asked God's forgiveness, I was set free instantly from their bonds. Fear, anger and selfishness were others that had to go. Jesus shed His blood that I might be free from them. I have had temptations in some of these areas once in a great while, but I am completely free from their control—it is as if a great heavy load has been lifted from my body.

I have emphasized my mental or emotional attitudes because I think they are often more important to God than some other bondages, but I really believe that *anything* that stands between us and God *must* be dealt with if we are honest with ourselves and mean business with God. God sends His Holy Spirit to bring conviction in your heart. And so it was with my smoking habit; this happened during my pregnancy, too.

I had smoked for twenty years and, frankly, could see nothing evil or sinful in the practice even though most of my Christian friends didn't do it. It was a practice that I had seen was indulged in by some very "nice" people as I grew up. For me it was quite a normal thing to do, sort of like the morning habit of drinking coffee. Even though I hadn't stopped smoking for any length of time, I could go for a matter of a day or more, and certainly many hours, without a cigarette, so fancied myself in complete control of my habit. It was a real shock when God showed me that I didn't have control, and that smoking, quite to the contrary, controlled me.

When I became the most defensive about my smoking, God was able to get my attention in this area. Suddenly there was a drastic change, and that which I smugly thought had been so controllable became obviously the opposite. I found myself smoking more and more and realizing I had a fight on my hands that I hadn't seemed to have before. If I'd run out of cigarettes, even in the late evening hours, I'd beg Rich to get out of bed and drive around looking for another pack, asking forgiveness all the while. I had never had to resort to this before in all the previous twenty years, and I was mortified! I can still picture poor Rich struggling into his trousers after settling comfortably into bed for his relaxation after a tiring day. He was so patient and accommodating with me, and that finally crowned my conviction with action.

I asked God how I could get free. He told me to go to the ladies' prayer group I attended weekly and ask for prayer. (I might interject here that I have found that God chooses to work in different ways for each situation. It's a good idea to ask Him how He wants to handle each one and then be receptive to His answer.) When I sat in their "prayer chair" and voiced my request, they were thrilled. So many of them had been through the same struggle. They laid hands on me and asked God to free me from my habit, then thanked Him for doing so. It was as simple as that. No yelling deliverance session; no wailing or crying—just an attitude of joy and rejoicing. It almost seemed as though nothing had happened.

One of the ladies said that while we were praying she had a vision of an apple. She didn't really know what it meant, but she guessed that if I craved a cigarette in the future I should eat an apple to rid myself of the temptation. I took this as from the Lord; but I was never around an apple when I was tempted to smoke! So I would picture one in my mind and, sure enough, the desire would leave me instantly. In time the temptations became fewer and farther between. Each time I resisted, it became easier to resist the next time. I came to believe that the vision of the apple was God's reminder to me of Adam and Eve's temptation in the Garden of Eden. Because it has blessed and helped me, I pass it on to those of you who are suffering from a temptation. God always provides a way out of temptation, never giving us more than we can bear (1 Cor. 10:13).

There isn't any shackle from which Jesus won't set us free, no matter how horrible or impossible it may seem to us. We must be willing to repent, sincerely turning from it, and then cooperate with God in turning the problem over to Him. Sometimes He will just lift it from us in the privacy of our homes; and sometimes He chooses to use another person or persons to pray for us. We have to realize that there's no place for embarrassment or pride. We will be set free on *God's terms* and *not ours.*

Our strength and victory lie in daily submitting every area of our lives to the Lordship of Jesus Christ, and then there is nothing for which there is no solution. Nothing is impossible with God!

*   *   *

We planned and waited for that third child with great excitement. I read some Christian books on childbirth and was convinced that I could have a painless delivery, just like the books said. I suffered very little in childbirth before and, now that I was a Christian, I felt I shouldn't have to suffer at all. After a few weeks I even talked Rich into being in the delivery room with me for the first time! I had it all figured out—how wonderful it was going to be.

It *was* wonderful, but it was wonderful the way *God* planned it—*not* the way *I* planned it!

I went into labor a full month before my due date at around 5:00 in the morning. I casually called the doctor, who just as casually suggested I drive out to the hospital "in case." I took my time getting my things together and then awakened Rich. The poor man almost fell over himself trying to get dressed and race out the door. I got the same reaction one might get by yelling "fire" in a crowd. I still laugh thinking about the picture he made.

When we got to the hospital a half hour later, I was still very comfortable; but almost the minute I lay down in the labor room, the contractions hit me like a sledgehammer with a painful power I've never experienced before or since. They caught me so off guard, and with such force, that I was unable even to pray. All I could do was try to breathe through my gasps and say once, "God, help me!" Immediately, He told me to have Rich pray for me.

"Honey, quick . . . pray for me . . . I can't do it myself," I managed desperately between contractions.

Rich began to pray in tongues. The Spirit does know how to make intercession when we don't. The pain subsided into a mild discomfort from that time on. God is best glorified in an impossible situation!

Nurses suddenly began to rush frantically about. The doctor wasn't there yet, and it appeared they would have to deliver the baby themselves. The labor had moved along much faster than anticipated (one cm. dilation to 10 cm. in 15 minutes!). Everyone looked worried, but Jesus had given me His "tranquilizer" and I felt peaceful.

I was being taken into the delivery room when the doctor flew past me to get ready. As he ran by, he apologized to Rich. It looked as if it might be a complicated delivery, so the doctor preferred that Rich not be in there after all. I was disappointed but still not worried. After all, Jesus had taken over.

The breech delivery was difficult for the doctor because not only did the baby's legs have to be straightened and the body turned to allow for delivery, but one of the arms, which was wrapped around the neck, had to be disentangled, too. No wonder everything seemed to be taking so long!

I'm sure the doctor was most relieved when he finally delivered a precious baby girl. She was a hefty 7 lbs. 4 ozs. despite being a month early, and looked healthy and normal. After two boys, a girl was a welcome treat—how perfect! We named her Amy, which means beloved. Her dad couldn't have been more pleased, and he whispered words of gratitude and pride as they wheeled me into the recovery room. They told Rich I would be sleeping then, so he went home to rest and to tell the boys our good news. They hadn't even been awake when we left the house.

I would love to have fallen off into a deep sleep then, and could easily have done so if a nurse hadn't taken my blood pressure every fifteen minutes. I resigned myself quickly to the fact that I wouldn't get any sleep until I went to my own room, and I counted the minutes to make the time go faster. My little game was interrupted by a male voice.

"Mrs. Life?"

"Yes, that's me."

"I'm the pediatrician you arranged for to check your baby after delivery. May I sit down?"

CHAPTER 10

Resident Physician

I hadn't been out of the delivery room more than an hour, and here was this doctor telling me that our new daughter needed medical treatment. I received the news calmly, and I can only surmise that God gave me His peace in abundance when I needed it.

Our baby was born with a congenital hip dislocation—the whole hip bone was out of the socket and the socket was abnormally open. The cure, with verification by an orthopedic specialist, was to be months and possibly a year or more in a cast and braces to force the hip into place and then waiting for the socket to close over it to form safe and normal joint action.

Another complication was a jaundiced condition caused by my R-H negative blood factor. I hadn't noticed it when I saw her, but her skin had a definite yellow cast to it. The pediatrician assured me that with a series of special light treatments, her skin should reach normal coloring and the condition should be cured by the time she went home. This proved to be accurate.

The orthopedic specialist we brought her to on our return home verified the pediatrician's diagnosis; and at the age of eleven days, Amy went into another hospital overnight to have applied the first of a "series of casts." When we came to pick her up the next day, we were surprised to find that the cast went from under her arms, down over her lower body front and back, and all the way to the ends of both of her feet. There was a small hole left for changing cut-up strips of tiny paper diapers. It wasn't until then, looking at this tiny, helpless little bundle of baby, that I began to realize the severity of her problem.

She had been given twelve pairs of booties and little shoes as gifts—really an incredible amount—and it looked as if she would never wear them. Everyone I spoke to seemed to have a relative or friend who had been born with the same problem, and each story involved many months—a year and sometimes two—of casts and braces.

From the beginning of Amy's problems Rich and I turned to God for our answers. For a time there was pleading; for a time, anger; then questions; but finally, thanks. Thanks? He was still God, and He knew what He was allowing was for good and would somehow be used to His glory (Rom. 8:28). If we believed God's Word, we had to trust. Sometimes, quite frankly, it was difficult; only with Jesus was it ever made easy.

We were told by the doctor when Amy's cast was put on that she would go into another one in three weeks to allow for growth. The day before this change was due, I heard that Kenneth Hagin was in town, giving a series of teachings and praying afterwards for the sick. I knew of him through some of the books he had written and I trusted his ministry. I felt so strongly that God wanted us to take Amy for prayer that evening, and Rich quietly agreed.

Rich held Amy as we stood in the prayer line. I don't remember Rev. Hagin's exact words as he laid his hands on Amy, but I was deeply touched and felt the power of God more strongly than I can convey in words.

During that day I had seen an image in my mind that I

had dismissed as being rather "Hollywood and dramatic." It was of Amy's cast breaking down the middle and falling off when she was healed—sort of like a Cecil B. DeMille Bible movie, so I hadn't even told Rich.

But the next morning, when I got up to change and feed Amy, I found her cast *breaking apart down the middle!* I couldn't believe it and yet there was no denying what I actually saw. I had a tremendous surge of faith that was confirmed when Rich came home and admitted that he had had exactly the same vision!

I called the doctor right away about the broken cast, but he reinforced it instead of removing it. Because she still had growing space, the cast wasn't removed nor were X rays taken until she had been in it for four weeks. When the doctor finally checked her and the X rays, he declared in amazement that she was healed, but he didn't say more. I found out later from some of his staff members that Amy's miracle was the talk of the office. Praise the Lord!

When I look back on the situation I see how Jesus was so glorified in her healing. I was asked to write an article for our church magazine and the Lord told me to tell this story about Amy. When it was published, the full story had to be condensed because of the limited space. Rich then suggested that we put it in flyer form—it wouldn't be too expensive to run some complete ones off for out-of-town relatives and friends. He had 500 printed then, and I couldn't imagine what we'd do with that many. We are now approaching the 4,000 mark. Somehow it has gotten all over the world to com_ort and encourage many who face the same problem with alarm! We are grateful to God that He, years later, is still using Amy to lift up Jesus.

In nine short months Amy battled with a constant succession of illnesses. When she was nine months old we faced another crisis.

She awoke that morning with a runny nose and soon

wasn't able to hold down any food or liquids. By noon her fever was up to 103°, so I called her doctor who said to bring her right into the office.

"I would suggest she enter the hospital immediately," he said on examining Amy. "She is infected from the top of her head to the tips of her toes, you might say." I can still hear those words, cutting through me with fear.

Her eyes were running, her throat raw, her ears infected, her lungs full of fluid, and her white blood count alarmingly high. "Bronchial pneumonia" said the report. It had come on her very fast and with tremendous force to an already weakened body.

In the hospital they put her in an oxygen tent, and we went home in a daze to wait. Our boys had never been hospitalized, and now our daughter was being treated in a hospital for the third time in the first nine months of her life. It was something we had never had to face before, and we were really worried.

That evening, to be alone in prayer, I knelt beside Amy's empty crib and found myself crying out to God, "Father, you gave Amy to us and we've loved her so much. We dedicated her life to you from the beginning and so she really belongs to you. You've allowed this illness to happen for some good reason that I don't know now. I am asking you for her healing, but if you choose to take her home to you now, I'll accept it as your will. If she lives, though, I ask again that you use her life that she might live to glorify Jesus. Amen."

I hadn't planned the words ahead of time, but they flowed with real sincerity from the very depths of my being. I meant every word because I trusted God. Her welfare was something that was now out of my hands. I was placing her, in spirit, in God's hands where she really belonged and I could only wait to see how He would work.

Amy came home four days later and the doctor told my husband that he had never seen a more "incredible breakthrough" from such a serious condition as Amy experienced her *first night* in the hospital!

When we give our burdens to Jesus and step out of the way, giving Him thanks and praise, then He does His glorious work unhindered. Even Amy knows this. I've never seen such faith as she has had even before she could talk. If she falls or hurts herself, she asks for prayer right away, and it's exciting to see how fast the pain leaves or how quickly the healing takes place. Her face has always glowed at the mention of the name of Jesus. It's as if she really knows Him personally.

*   *   *

Jesus is really our family's "Resident Physician," and He has blessed us many times with His healing touch. We try to be aware of the fact that He can choose many methods to show His healing hand, and we must be careful to be led by His Spirit for each individual case. The Bible speaks of anointing with oil, the laying on of hands, prayer and fasting, and prayer at a geographical distance. And, of course, God also uses doctors to perform His healing grace! I have even learned there can be healing through the Sacrament of Communion.

The month before Amy's pneumonia bout, we were driving back from an Easter visit with Rich's family in Ohio and I noticed that my back was starting to bother me. I decided I must have pulled something when I tried to take care of the baby in the car on the way home. I thought that it would go away if I ignored it (never having had back trouble before), but by the third day, I went to bed and stayed there another two days. The pain in my lower back had spread down my left leg and, on the sixth day, Rich had to help me into the office of our family doctor. He discovered that the reflexes in my left leg were gone, so advised immediate hospitalization for complete rest and tests. It was difficult leaving the family alone, but I was in such pain that it was impossible for me to be of help to them anyway, so I agreed.

The doctor decided to postpone the difficult tests in favor of traction and therapy in addition to medication to relax me and dull the pain. For almost two weeks, I didn't see any improvement and we still didn't know for sure what was wrong with me, though the doctor suspected a muscle spasm. Whatever it was, I was almost helpless. I had a baby and two boys at home who needed me, as well as a dear, overworked husband who never once complained.

"Would you like to take Communion?" The nurses' aide asked one night for the first time. It was a denominational hospital with a strong spiritual atmosphere.

"Would I? Oh, I'd so appreciate it, but I don't think they'll let me. You see, I'm not a member of that church."

"I'll see, Mrs. Life. You never know."

I really got my hopes up until the clergyman came into the room looking so apologetic that I knew what he was going to say before he said it.

"I'm so sorry, but I just can't serve you Communion. I hope you understand, but that is part of our official stand. You must belong to our church to receive."

"I'm sorry, too, but to be frank, I don't understand. All I can think of is that Jesus told His followers to take it in remembrance of Him. I think of myself as His follower first, not an official member of any particular denomination." I was so disappointed that I was almost in tears. The poor man, who was just following orders, looked embarrassed and quickly left, repeating a hurried apology on the way.

One of our church members who heard my story over the phone suggested that if I really wanted Communion that badly, our pastor could administer it to me in the hospital. Never having had experience in this area, it hadn't occurred to me even to think of it, and I was overjoyed when the pastor walked into my room the next day with his wife and his Communion kit. The Lord had filled me with a real hunger to get closer to Him through Communion.

It was such a beautiful time—the three of us alone with Jesus. From that time on the pain began to leave, my back loosened up, and the next morning I felt fine for the first time in over three weeks. I was discharged in a couple of days when the doctor was sure it would last.

The doctor might say that I was healed because of treatment, but I am sure that Jesus touched me during that Communion and that it was His blood and body that took my pain and infirmity on the cross (Isa. 53:5; 1 Pet. 2:24). The medical doctor and his staff tried, but Jesus was the Great Physician who worked the final cure.

*　　*　　*

When we put Jesus on call as our Resident Physician, we found that He even took care of our dog! We had a good example of this when we built a balcony on the second-story level of our house shortly before Amy was born.

"The only thing that concerns me," I told Rich one day, "is that the dog might go over the edge. And then later on, the baby. It's so far down, honey." I was referring to Craig's pet dachshund puppy who was only a few months old and quite small. Rich assured me he'd put some wire around the balcony railing for added protection but, like so many household chores, it kept getting put off and finally forgotten.

Sure enough, I walked out on the balcony one day and, in an effort to get out of my way, the poor puppy backed right over the edge. I could see sheer panic in his little black eyes as he struggled helplessly to get a foothold just before he went down. I heard him smash onto the cement patio beneath with such force that he bounced up into the grass a few feet away. I was sure that he was dead. How could a tiny creature suffer a two-story fall like that and live?

Craig heard the commotion by this time, and I led him into the living room while his dad and brother went down to get the dog. They couldn't believe it, but Fritz was actually alive. They hurried him into the car and as they headed for the vet's office, I told Craig we should pray. There didn't seem to be anything I could say to comfort him then, so we had to put his dear smashed pet into God's hands.

It was a simple prayer asking God to please restore our Fritz. We loved him and couldn't bear to see him suffer. Craig joined me in a brave "Amen."

Moments later Rich and Jim returned. Fritz not only survived the fall, but the doctor couldn't find a thing wrong with him—not one broken bone or even a cut! Jesus had been so faithful.

*   *   *

Another way that Jesus heals is by letting us stand in faith without seeing the results instantly.

I had fallen badly while running across a bumpy street, ripping my knee open so severely that it affected the nerve endings and left a numbness even after the wound finally healed. I had caught the full weight of the fall with my right hand and arm, and I must have pulled something in my shoulder. From that time on I suffered terrible pain in that shoulder, pain that would extend down my whole arm, at worst; at best, a nagging sensation of burning at the joint. Sometimes the pain was so severe that I had trouble sleeping, and I found simple tasks like putting on a coat difficult. I didn't think a doctor could do anything for it, so I never did consult one. I had Rich pray for me when the pain got unbearable and it would go away each time but then come back eventually.

This had gone on for about a year and a half when we found ourselves in a healing service conducted much like Kathryn Kuhlman's. It was in Tulsa, Oklahoma, and the minister in this case was a lovely young woman by the name of Vicki Jamison. She used to be a part of Kenneth Hagin's team, ministering in song, but God had since anointed her for a ministry of healing. She traveled the country seeing restoration through many miracles.

When we arrived at the meeting Mrs. Jamison had already sung, led in a worship time, and then built faith through a message from the Word. When the healing service began, Vicki called forth different illnesses as the Lord revealed them to her through a word of knowledge (1 Cor. 12:7-9), and each time she asked the person to which it applied to claim it by faith, raising his hand or standing up.

Suddenly I heard her say, "God is healing someone now, here, in the shoulder. It's probably bursitis."

I looked up and saw her pointing to the same area that had bothered me, and I noticed that she used the same medical term I had used in referring to the pain in my shoulder. I felt a "quickening" in my spirit, but that's all. There was no other sensation like "heat" or a feeling of "electricity" that often distinguishes a healing in a service of this kind. As a matter of fact, there was even a slight pain still there as usual.

I looked around thinking it must be a call for someone else, but no one raised his hand. I still felt a "quickening" in my spirit (a feeling I often get when God is trying to tell me something), so I raised my hand and claimed my healing by faith (it wasn't what I'd call really strong faith at that point).

For weeks I had to fight off the enemy's whispers in my ear that the healing was really for some "little old lady in the back who never had the nerve to raise her hand," and I'd have to say right back, "That isn't so. It was for me, and I was healed that night—New Year's Eve—no matter what you say!"

When the pain was severe, it was a bit harder to say, but I said it anyway—the same words each time, over and over. I had no proof other than the "feeling" I had in my spirit that God had meant the healing for me when Vicki called it out, and I knew that God *never* lies. The more I had to stand against Satan's symptoms, the stronger my faith grew. One day a few weeks after New Year's Eve, God honored that faith and removed the symptoms instantly and completely.

That was it—the end of the battle. I've never had even a twinge of pain in that area since then. Jesus just took it *all* away—every bit of it—and I testify to His glory.

*   *   *

I think there's always a special excitement about your first healing, even if the infirmity is not serious. A few years ago a wart developed on the pad of my thumb, right where it bothered me so much. Even though I had a deep assurance from the beginning that God could heal it, I quickly lost patience and had it removed surgically. It wasn't long before it came back—same spot and same size, fairly large. Again I had the same assurance that God would remove it supernaturally, and again a few months later I grew impatient with waiting and had it removed surgically.

By this time the scar was large, though the wart was gone. But, you guessed it, this time when it came back, it grew larger than ever and began to give me pain, which it had not done before.

One day I was having an especially hard time manipulating the car's steering wheel because my thumb hurt so much. I just pulled over to the side of the road and began to talk to God.

"O.K., Lord, I give up. No more trying to remove it my way. It didn't work and now it's worse than ever. Forgive me for not trusting you. This time I'm going to wait for you to heal it, but please do it quickly because it hurts so much. Thank you, Lord. Amen."

I went on my way then and forgot my thumb. I didn't even think about it until the next day, and then when I looked at it I got the thrill of my life. The whole wart was *completely gone.* The only thing that remained was the scar to remind me that I hadn't trusted Him from the beginning.

*　　*　　*

The phone rang one day and a friend from church was on the line with some incredible news.

"You weren't in church last night, so I had to call and tell you what happened. It seems that Jim just got back from a trip to Florida and told us how God was moving in a new way down there, growing out short legs and arms. Well, Jim prayed for some people here and it always worked! He even prayed for me, and it was the most fantastic—"

"Now, wait a minute," I interrupted. "How ridiculous! Why on earth would God do this? It just isn't that important." (Note the self-righteousness.)

"But, Nancy, some people have a real serious problem in this area: clothes have to be specially made, custom shoes bought, and in some cases people live with pain because of this."

"I can see that. But didn't you say that Jim prayed for people like you who don't have any serious problem?"

"Sure," she answered patiently, "but I guess the point Jim was trying to make was that most everyone has a short arm or leg—we're all kind of imperfect, even by less than an inch—so God decided that this would be a wonderful way to build faith in each of us, both by having this experience ourselves and then by praying for others who could have it. You see, Jim prayed for only a couple of people and then he insisted that other believers could do it, too. This isn't a miracle that works through only a few. This is for the whole church of Christ!"

"I'd surely like to see it. Maybe that would help me to see the purpose of it," I said, still skeptical. I wasn't skeptical about the possibility, but I was still questioning the purpose. It didn't dawn on me that I was actually questioning God's wisdom!

During the next church service I was one of the first who went to the front for prayer. They sat me down, back pushed tight against the back of the pew, and lifted my legs so that they were straight out. Sure enough, when my heels were held tightly together, there was a definite difference in length. Imagine, I had never even known it!

Everyone gathered around as one of them held my legs out and feet together, and they told me to keep my eyes open and watch. All they said was, "Thank you, Lord, for growing out this leg. Thank you, Jesus. We praise you . . . ," and it wasn't more than a few seconds later that I felt my one leg pull out and saw it meet the other one so that now the two were exactly equal!

The sensation it stirred in my spirit can't be explained. My faith soared and my excitement flared. I felt very sorry all at once that I had doubted God's reasoning. I was witness to a real miracle right before my eyes, and it was actually happening to me as well as to many others around me! There was a noticeable difference as I stood to my feet and for the next few hours I felt a bit off balance. After all, one of my legs had grown out over a half an inch and I wasn't used to it yet!

I was then encouraged to pray for someone else. At first I felt so inadequate, but God quickly showed me by this experience that *Jesus* is the One who does it and *He* is *never* inadequate. Since then I have never doubted that this healing will be done if God leads me to pray for someone, and it never ceases to strengthen my faith and boldness.

Many people have been brought to a personal acceptance of Jesus as their Saviour because of this simple miracle. And a soul that is saved for the Kingdom of God proves God's wisdom as nothing else can.

CHAPTER 11

Precious Presents, Glorious Gifts

When one's life is committed to the Lordship of Jesus Christ, Satan does not like it, and he jumps at every chance he gets to vex and harass. The best intentions are often misunderstood, and your very closest relatives suddenly don't understand you anymore. When Jesus truly shines in your life, those who reject Him are going to be very uncomfortable with you. But Jesus said to expect these things because they happened to Him, too (John 15:18-21).

One couple Rich and I were especially close to and loved very much, and they loved the Lord too. Many times we talked about Jesus and shared scriptures to encourage and uplift them when the need arose. They hadn't studied the Bible in their church because it stressed a dependence on God through their clergy. They always seemed glad to learn about the promises in God's Word. We did not share with them about the baptism with the Holy Spirit—we were always honest about the charismatic church we attended. Slowly they saw less and less of us. Although they were sweet when we saw them, the change was obvious and the reason became more than clear. They were afraid because they didn't understand. I'm sure they didn't mean to hurt us, but we felt a deep sense of loss.

Sometimes people do more than just evade you. We have found ourselves the targets of harassment, business theft, malicious rumor with intent to destroy our reputation, telephone threats, and a planned attempt by a stranger to kill us with his car! We have wondered why we were considered so important a threat but know this is all part of the spiritual warfare Jesus warns us about. We don't battle flesh and blood, but Satan himself. Is this a cause for fear? NEVER, because God has given us His protective armor to ward off the darts of the enemy with new strength and purpose, all the while witnessing of the glory and salvation of Jesus Christ (Eph. 6:11-18).

But there is no need to dwell on the occasional harassments when our life in Jesus has given our family far more rewards in every way possible. Therefore, a chapter about the gifts God has given us is far more logical. There isn't *anything* He considers too small or unimportant to help with. I am reminded of the time we wanted to buy a pontoon boat.

We had saved $200 to buy this boat, something I'd always wanted; and with a lake so close to us it would be used often. We couldn't afford any more than $200, but even the oldest used boats were going for $400 and up that summer. We looked and looked from spring through August. We'd just about given up, deciding it wasn't God's will for us to have one. (Until then we hadn't thought about God in the matter, figuring not to bother Him with anything that minor, I suppose.) Rich and I have since found that *if it doesn't go against God's will for our lives,* He delights in giving us the desires of our hearts.

It was when we considered God's will in this matter of a pontoon boat that He intervened. We received a letter from a neighbor who heard we wanted one, and he said he'd sell us his used one for $100! Praise the Lord, He not only got us a perfect pontoon boat but with the price cut in half! And that's typical of our heavenly Father's special love!

Another time I was driving along thinking about a friend

who was moving to Maine from St. Paul. She originally came from New York, and we had had such fun talking about mutual friends and favorite places in our old home town. I was thinking about how I'd miss her, and I casually told the Lord I'd really like another "New York friend" to take her place. The following day at the next church service a woman got up and gave a testimony, and all I heard was her *New York accent*. After the service, I introduced myself, told her where I was from, and we embraced with a shout like long lost relatives. My Lord was so wonderful!

Then there was the neighborhood dog that had caused a lot of problems by being allowed to roam loose. He had bitten several people, and his barking was continuous and nerve-wracking. This dog was annoying as well as dangerous, and for too long I had worried and complained about him to no avail. When I finally asked God in serious prayer one day to please help me with this concern, the dog ran away and they never did find him! I had prayed for help, and this is the way God chose to meet the need. There isn't *anything* our heavenly Father won't take care of when we turn to Him for the solution.

*   *   *

And then there are the wonderfully large blessings seeing the lives of our children change in their new walk with the Lord.

As I told you, the boys had accepted Christ as their Saviour in 1969, the year we did. The Word of God promises that the gift of the Holy Spirit is for our children as well as for us (Acts 2:38,39), and it seemed only natural that the boys would experience this too.

When both of them were baptized in the Holy Spirit, that new dimension of fullness was added to their lives, and they experienced a new appreciation and love for God and what He wanted for them, as well as a new hunger to study His Word.

He provided a wonderful way to put all of this on a more solid foundation, directing us to send them to a Christian day school in Minneapolis. That's what God wanted for them, so He provided the tuition money every year for it. We didn't have the extra money when we sent them, but when God wants us to do something, He always provides a way to make it possible.

One day we heard from the school that Jim needed extra help with grammar. He hadn't had much background in this area in public school, and it was vital that he catch up with the class. The school suggested tutoring but couldn't supply us with the name of anyone who could do it.

Time went on and our search produced no willing or able names. In church one evening I brought it before the Lord in prayer. We needed someone fast because too much time had already elapsed, and someone inexpensive because we really couldn't afford the extra expense.

During the testimony time, a woman stood up and told how the Lord had moved to solve some of her problems as a school teacher. On impulse, after the service I asked her what subject she taught. I'm sure that you've guessed—English, and it was also exactly the grade Jim was in! When I asked her if she would be available to help Jim once a week, she said yes, and would pray about the charge. A few days later she told me that she would help Jim for *nothing* as unto the Lord!

Dorothy was instrumental in helping Jim pass English that year and, when the months were over, God provided us with some money to send her so we could show our deep appreciation.

Another story concerning Jim happened during the Viet Nam conflict. I was worried about his being drafted and going off to war. One day I approached God in prayer about it, begging Him not to let Jim go into the armed services or near a war.

God admonished me to be willing to relinquish Jim into

whatever walk God would choose, and to pray instead that Jim be "fully prepared by My Spirit" for that service.

I prayed then as God directed. It wasn't too long after that that he began to cultivate an interest in Oral Roberts University in Tulsa, Oklahoma, where there is a strong emphasis on the work of the Holy Spirit. I felt this was a direct answer to prayer.

The next step was trying to get in—which, right until he was finally accepted, looked like a losing battle. His grades had been too low until his senior year when he had made a tremendous effort to pull them up. Though I lost hope, Jim never did. He said that this school was the one where God wanted him to go, and he never even applied anywhere else. When he got the letter of acceptance, Jim was able to say, "I told you so," and we were grateful to God for making it possible. The spiritual atmosphere is evident when one walks on the ORU campus—it should be a perfect place for that "preparation in the Spirit" God has in mind.

When Craig was born again at age eight, I saw a nice quiet boy turn on fire for Jesus. He suddenly had a burning desire to share His Saviour with everyone. He started inviting the little neighborhood children into our backyard where he'd open a big picture Bible and read to them.

One day when we were out, he made little "bookmarks" with Bible verses on them and put them in several of the neighbors' mailboxes. His excitement was something that God turned on inside of him—we had nothing to do with it—and it was a joy to watch. We wondered what he'd come up with next!

He started making little crosses out of paper, cardboard, and then wood. The wooden ones got larger and larger—one day he had a terrible time dragging into the house something he had made in the garage. When he set it against the wall and got out of the way, we saw it was a cross as big as Craig himself and on it a cardboard Jesus he had painted! We didn't really have any room for it, but there was so much love that went into the making of that cross that I couldn't throw it out (I still have it!).

* * *

Another "precious present" God gave us concerned Rich's parents. They were nice people—generous and likable—but had avoided anything "religious" in favor of a Christmas and Easter visit to church. The church the family had always gone to was one of those "socially acceptable" churches, where the minister didn't talk about a personal relationship with Jesus.

After Rich and I were born again and then baptized with the Holy Spirit, we tried to share these experiences with Rich's folks. They thought we were on a "new kick" that would pass to something else in time. They saw the change in us but had no way of understanding. They were glad for us, but they didn't want to get "fanatic." We kept praying.

When we heard that Billy Graham was going to have a crusade in Cleveland, we sent for tickets for the folks. Maybe hearing the good news from someone else would make a difference. But God was already working in their hearts and they had made their own plans to go. We got a call from them the next day. They had both accepted Christ during the altar call the night before! Having suffered through the excruciating summer heat for hours, they went forward to accept the suffering of Christ for their own personal salvation. Praise the Lord—we are now truly one family, born by His Spirit.

* * *

I encourage you to ask God for every need and desire in your life, knowing that you have a heavenly Father who really cares. Matthew 11:22-26 is probably the most concise teaching on the subject of prayer.[1] His Word says we may ask *anything we desire, believing* that God will answer. Faith is vital in the Christian walk. It is the evidence that we know God is real and will answer prayer, always standing behind His promises.

If we find that God is not answering prayer, we need to search our hearts to see if we are harboring any bitterness or unforgiveness toward anyone. These attitudes will hinder and block answers to prayer.

So dare to trust God to meet *every* need in *every* situation no matter how small or large the request. There is no "but . . ." to God's promises. He doesn't waiver and He doesn't lie. He is just waiting for you to ask.

---

[1]Also see Matthew 21:22; Mark 9:23; John 14:13-15; and James 4:3, for further references on how to pray.

CHAPTER 12

As the Spirit Leads

I was sitting in church, singing with the rest of the congregation one night, when God broke into my spirit with these words,

"You won't be here much longer."

I knew it was God. The Bible says His children will know His voice, and I knew it was God. But I also didn't like what I heard. I was so happy in that church; the people were such a comfort and help to me that I didn't see how I could go on then without their guidance and support. I loved and depended on this fellowship. Tears came to my eyes, but I quickly comforted myself with the knowledge that maybe it was my imagination after all. I dried the tears and went back to singing. Then . . . "You won't be here much longer."

The same words were called out to my heart, and again I felt tears come to my eyes. Finally I told God that although I wasn't willing, I was willing to be made willing! As attached as I was to that church body, I never felt at home there from that night on. It was as if I had already been separated from them in the spirit. God had instantly begun a work in my heart.

I didn't know exactly what God's word to me meant, whether it referred to leaving that church or the city or the state, but I had a feeling that it would be a bigger move than I realized at the time. Then God began to work in Rich, and both of us sensed a relocation of some kind. It bothered us at first to think of a state move because Rich's company was well established in St. Paul, his stockholders and board of directors were located in the Twin Cities. Moving a family is hard enough, but a whole company was awesome to think about.

Then God began a spiritual healing in Rich's life, and he learned about that hard, but vital, death-to-self that God had already begun to take me through six months earlier. Now we were in the battle together and God worked to unify us through this as never before. We struggled, and learned, and struggled, and learned—but now together in strength and purpose as never before. Little by little God formed a deeper unity between us that was to solidify our marriage as well as our family life as a whole. We faced a lot of correction in many areas that affected not only our relationship with each other, but with the children too. When God's light shines on the things you have hidden away (sometimes even from yourself), the contrast between the good and the bad is glaringly obvious. In time the Lord leaves nothing that must be dealt with unrevealed if you have a humble spirit that desires God's best and God's will for your life. And then He gently, lovingly guides and helps to cleanse and heal each mistake—each wounded relationship.

It was during this time that God showed us that we had a calling on our lives and that God had taken us very literally when we asked to be "emptied and used." We had totally committed ourselves into His service, and we sat back to wait for God to show us how He meant to use us. A new walk was beginning.

By June we were pretty sure we would be moving, but we didn't know when or how or why. God had blessed us financially, so we planned a trip west, and set out across country hoping God would point out along the way where He might relocate us. By the time we got back home a month later, having gone west to California by the southern route and home via the northern route, we still didn't have a clue. The only thing was that we had been really excited about the spiritual atmosphere in Tulsa where Jim planned on going to college at ORU, and felt more at ease than ever about sending him there.

In addition to our church, Rich and I had been regular in attendance at the Full Gospel Business Men's Fellowship International, a charismatic fellowship that meets monthly in our area. Many Christian speakers—laymen and ministers—present the message of salvation and the work of the Holy Spirit in the meetings. Through this group we met an evangelist from Tulsa, and we talked seriously about working together. It seemed an exciting opportunity to join an already established ministry, but it would be a serious commitment, so we entered into many months of prayer about it. It was tempting, and it was God's work, but we wanted to be *sure* that it was God's work for *us*. Was this what *God* intended, or what *we* desired? We prayed that God would show us His will in a move to Tulsa, possibly to work with this ministry. We prayed that He would open the right doors and close the wrong ones.

We heard that Kenneth Hagin's Evangelistic Association was starting a new training school for people who had a call of God on their lives. Rich applied for entrance and was accepted. (Wives were later invited to attend classes with their husbands, giving me a priceless opportunity for study.) The school called RHEMA Bible Training Center was in Tulsa, Oklahoma! Too many things seemed to point our paths to Tulsa, so we went ahead with plans for a move there for the school year. We began to see why God, several months before, had put the desire to relocate in our hearts.

Rich decided to honor his commitment to God's service in a further way, and put his company up for sale. If it sold, fine; if it didn't, fine. Whatever God wanted—He would do it the best way and in the right time. Rich had cherished his company and the work with it, but if God had the kind of plans we thought He might, Rich knew he must at least be willing to give up his company if it was God's desire to free Rich's time for other things. We knew God would show us because we had asked Him to.

When we'd question the wisdom of the move (there was a tremendous spiritual warfare), God would intervene with confirmation over and over. And God sent friends to counsel and encourage when the warfare reached its peaks.

Miracle after miracle was performed to pave the way for our move as Satan battled against us over and over. Only the love, support and prayers of some of our Christian friends—and some strangers—brought us over the rough spots. The Lord also joined us with a fellowship that sent us to Tulsa with their blessings and prayer support just like the ministries that went out in the New Testament days. It is very comforting to know that a body of God's people is totally with us in spirit as we walk into our new life. The pastor especially ministered so much encouragement and strength to us through the early trials, and we praise God for the burdens He places on fellow Christians' hearts for others in their times of need.

We tried to sit quietly back and let the Lord move as He willed. One day we got a call from Norfolk, Virginia—the Christian Broadcasting Network.[1] They wondered if we'd be available for an interview on their first live show of the "700 Club" from channel 44 in Chicago, Pat Robertson interviewing. It was incredible. Someone who had met us very briefly had given our names—we had no reputation at all. Again we felt God had arranged it. Our appearance on the show on March 14 proved an exciting experience.

---

[1]Read about CBN and God's work in TV in the book *Shout It From the Housetops,* by Pat Robertson (Pub., Logos).

Slowly we got calls for private counsel and prayer, working as a couple—as well as speaking dates both in and out of town. God was arranging it, and every time it was a wonderful learning process as well as a deep blessing.

We have made many moves in our married life together, but this is the first one Rich and I have placed entirely in God's hands. We have told Him we want to be in His service, and we don't really know for sure what that will prove to be. But we do know that we trust Him to prepare us and then lead us as He wills.

How could I be afraid in His hands when Jesus has freed me from the gutter of alcoholism and the despair of suicide—and set my feet upon His narrow path? He has made me willing to give up anything for Him—after all, He gave up everything for me. There isn't one tear I have shed that He hasn't wiped away; there isn't one burden He will not take up for me; there isn't any need He will not fill. What a mighty God we serve.

Apart from Him I can do nothing, for in myself I am unable and unworthy. There is nothing I want to do except as the Spirit leads.

So, move over, Mountain. There's work to be done, the harvest is ready, and nothing is impossible with God.